GREEN MACKINAW

IN EUROPE 1954-55

Alfred H. Siemens

Suite 300 - 990 Fort St
Victoria, BC, V8V 3K2
Canada

www.friesenpress.com

Copyright © 2017 by Alfred H. Siemens

First Edition — 2017

My warm appreciation to Rob Stuart of Austin Works for permission to use #44 (Austin A40 – on p. 41 of draft with images), to Dirk Detweiler for permission to include the picture of his father Bob Detweiler (#73 on p.60) and to the Jewish Historical Society of British Columbia for the right to reproduce the portrait of Dr. B.C. Binning (#9, p. 12) who was photographed by Fred S. Schiffer [October 8, 1966]. Jewish Museum and Archives of BC, L.24847.

All rights reserved.

No part of this publication may be reproduced in any form, or by any means, electronic or mechanical, including photocopying, recording, or any information browsing, storage, or retrieval system, without permission in writing from FriesenPress.

ISBN

978-1-4602-9533-5 (Hardcover)
978-1-4602-9534-2 (Paperback)
978-1-4602-9535-9 (eBook)

1. BIOGRAPHY & AUTOBIOGRAPHY, PERSONAL MEMOIRS

Distributed to the trade by The Ingram Book Company

THE DAYS OF THE YEAR

SOME PRELIMINARIES ... 1
Imagery — 3
A diary — 5
Additional materials — 7
Memory — 8
Early studies at UBC — 9

FRIDAY, SEPTEMBER 24, 1954 ... 13
Departure — 13
Additional money — 14
Crossing my country — 16
A modest ship with a colourful history — 19

THURSDAY, OCTOBER 14: ENGLAND ... 23
Anglophilia — 23
Filming with stills — 26
Beavering — 34
Oxbridge pilgrimages — 38
Looping south from London — 41

SATURDAY, OCTOBER 30: HAMBURG ... 46
'Die Freie und Hanzestadt Hamburg' — 46
'Hummel, Hummel' — 48
Dammtor — 49
Ground bricks and glass — 52
'Wer hätte das gedacht…' — 54
'Practically lifeless and continually losing ground' — 56
'Wenn der Hahn kräht auf dem Mist' — 62
Fifteen curtain calls — 66

An apparition	67
Movies	67
Other serious things	67
O Tannenbaum	69
Regret	70
International student	71
Lüneburger Heide	74

MONDAY, FEBRUARY 28, 1955 78

'Kennst du das Land wo die Zitronen blühn?'	78
Nothing left to say	80
Diligent again	84
Shoe leather for Florence	87
Uneven arches	92
Shadows high on the walls and men muttering in their dreams	94
Poste Restante	95
'Music Hour'	102
Money in Brindizi	103
Cut slopes	109

TUESDAY, MARCH 29, 1955, GREECE 111

Sauntering	111
Doric, Ionic and Corinthian	116
A grubby excursion	121
Intimations of Byzantium in Athens	125
Onto the Peninsula, just	127
Oliver	132
A crazy final Athenian week	134

SATURDAY, APRIL 16: BACK TOWARD HAMBURG 136

Another Easter	136
Approach to the Balkans	140
Viennese Woods	144

'Kulturstöber' 145
Across the northern foothills of the Alps 150
Castling 157
A particular bell 160
Deviation 162
Jim Draper 163
'Die grosse Dummheit' 166
Sprint 168
Foxhole reflections 170
'Stone book of history' 172
'Drink, drink, drink ...' 173
'Hier stehe ich, ich kann nicht anders' 174
Thumbing 175
Re-entry 176
The virginal slide show 179

SATURDAY, MAY 25: PENTECOST PUTTER 181
Enlarging my store 184
Wood 188

WEDNESDAY, JUNE 8: CONCLUDING EARLY 194
Evaluation 199
Last look around 201
Suddenly Denmark 206
Full circle 209

SUNDAY, JULY 3: LIFT OFF 212

ACKNOWLEDGEMENTS 215

ENDNOTE 216

About The Author

Alfred H. Siemens, PhD, is a professor emeritus in the Geography Department at the University of British Columbia. From the early 1990's he has been lecturing and conducting graduate seminars at various Mexican universities and research institutes. He is also an avid photographer, some of his work can be found at **www.landscapephotoart.com**

Mackinaw:

Wikipedia informs us (and where would we be without such a source of quick answers to everything) that a short coat of heavy water-repellent woollen cloth, usually plaid, is a "marker of [Canadian] national identity and working-class values, and has been exploited for effect in Canadian comedy shows."[1] Such a coat was excellent deck wear on the voyage across the North Atlantic in October and chic enough for my kind of skiing in the Harz Mountains a few months later. From the window of my room on the second floor of Papenkamp 16 in Hamburg I could see a recycling system working in the lane: one can for garbage and another for things that were still useful. People came along to check the latter. Before departure I put various pieces of clothing in the second bin, including a well-worn green mackinaw.

SOME PRELIMINARIES

    During the dark and wet winter months from 2011 to 2012, when a first draft of this memoir had already been written, I was stalled, not sure how to proceed. Who was I writing for? How should I represent myself? Was I doing justice to a pivotal year? Why should I bother? Alice, my wife, and I looked from North Vancouver to the slightly drier and sunnier parts of the southwest of British Columbia and went for several trips of distraction. On Vancouver Island we chanced on some stunning forest stands. One, just back of a beach, had been killed by salt water ponding around the roots. I was surrounded by pleasing forms, infinite branchings, plays of light and a wide range of tones – visual jazz.

    Trees have been stimulating photographic subjects for much of my life. I look up amazed at branches, most eloquent when they're bare. A forest green abstraction is on the cover of this book; it will be explained later. Trees intrigued me in Hamburg in the winter of 1954–55 before I left for the Mediterranean. An image of trees and spires begins the account of the year abroad. Knots and jagged limbs hinted at bomb damage, considerably healed by 1954, a dozen years after the air raids of WWII. The city centre itself had already been mostly rebuilt.

    By mid-April of 2012, my way of responding to aesthetic stimuli in the landscape and then processing what I had found, the making of images not for teaching, not for illustration, just for my soul, had had its usual restorative effect. I was able to regain my nerve and bear down on the rewriting of *GREEN MACKINAW*.

The making of this book has brought me a re-appreciation of a brief shining time. I've savored its adventures again, caught an echo of the earnest spirituality that pervaded the life of the young man and reflected on what came before and after. It was a surprise, here well into my retirement from Geography at the University of British Columbia, to see how an academic interest was taking shape in 1954–55 and a satisfaction to see that it had remained fairly coherent. All that is self-indulgent, of course, but I also offer the account as a gift to my family and friends. I know from the reactions of those who have been kind enough to read early versions that these recollections can resonate.

A study year in Europe, utterly common now, was still quite rare among my cohort at UBC and an astonishment in my home community of Abbotsford. It was not as audacious as a trip some Aussie friends undertook: they bought a taxi in London and headed for Katmandu, or indeed as eventful as the journey of my good friend Jim Draper from Capetown to Cairo, but for me the diagonal I traced through Europe in 1954–55 took on its own bright aura.

Memoirs are tricky business, often acidly reviewed. For someone ready to take the risk, there's the pleasure of wordsmithing, beyond that an opportunity for personal winnowing, a possibility for explanation. It's important to avoid aspersions and embarrassment, to find palatable ways to refer to oneself. I just couldn't take the young man too seriously, yet it seemed imperative to keep faith with what was recorded, to credit again what was felt and intended. Sometimes I approved of him, often I did not. In places I had to treat him with irony but usually I remained intrigued. I often contended with him, all this to bear the gaucherie of one's youth while re-savouring the adventure.

Alfred H. Siemens

I meant to avoid pedantries, to flout book-making conventions in form and content, I'd had quite enough of them. Call up my CV to gauge my long obeisance. However, the academic conditioning of a lifetime was not easily shaken off, especially the high regard for evidence prevalent in the social science disciplines that I frequented. This memoir thus inevitably became less of an imaginative improvisation and more of an investigation. Also, as the prospect of an actual submission for publication loomed, as my willful draft had to be made printable, I found myself succumbing to more and more conventions, including a frank and pre-emptive introductory review of sources.

Imagery

My collection of photographs has often seemed monstrous, unoverseeable. In 2008, I began the latest attempt at a reordering and soon came again on the images produced in Europe in 1954–55: packets of black and white negatives and prints, as well as two metal boxes of colour transparencies. The prints were shuffled back and forth and one after another the transparencies were held to a light. Such handling releases recollections as rubbing herbs releases scents. I remembered the awful moment in the early summer of 1955, it's almost funny now, coming back up from my trip into Italy and Greece, when I nearly lost the film exposed up to that point.

There are about three hundred images in this book, most are photographs from my store of negatives and positives as well as scans of materials in my files and in my library. I sought out enhancements on the web, out of the public domain or with explicit permission, and endnoted them. Sometimes I just needed an elaboration, like the image of a particular old car, or the face of a good friend I had not seen since 1955.

The images are not relegated to the role of strictly corseted and neatly captioned direct illustrations but have been invited to evoke, to make their own points. They may suggest something and then come back later to elaborate, they reflect emphasis and help spin associations with what came before or after.

The most satisfying aspect of the making of this book has been the grooming of the images. Some of them come from small originals of low resolution. For most of 1954–55 I had only a very basic 35mm camera, no zoom, no long and short lenses, no lovely German mechanism; all that came later. Successive groups of images were digitized, cropped, and had their blemishes removed. They could be lightened or darkened, enlivened in colour and contrast. Sometimes lines and textures could be sharpened, given just that extra edge. Disturbing objects, like a rock or a branch, could be taken out. If this is falsification, so be it. I consider it enhancement.

The facing page offers a taste of the restrained image manipulation throughout the book. It's what I do with all the photographic raw material that I select to print. It's from my "Pentecostal Putter", a ramble on a motorized bicycle (a 'moped') in

Green Mackinaw

May of 1955 through a good bit of was then West Germany. I'm in some small place, fascinated as usual with the buildings around me. The image at the top is as it came from self-rolled Ektachrome, developed in Zürich, as I found it in one of the metal boxes sixty years after the taking. It had faded and reddened (The Kodachrome that I also used fared much better.) In the second image the contrast has been strengthened, the red reduced and the vibrancy of all the other colours heightened; the fodder has been made really green.

Alfred H. Siemens

It was satisfying not only to enhance images but to lay down pleasing pages. Text in a clean open Century Gothic font was juxtaposed with the pictures and the whole was shuffled repeatedly, like domino players shuffle bones between games. This helped me to realize some visual inclinations, manipulate emphasis, reduce sprawl and develop associations. Images could be left in colour or converted to black and white, perhaps given a tint. I experimented with cropping and repetition. Here and there I pushed against the iron casements of the usual margins. Who knows how much of all of this will survive publication; some marks of my struggles will probably be apparent.

There are fifteen maps in this book. I don't think I could write a book without maps. A lifetime in Geography does that to you. They are fetishes for me, that is objects to which I am devoted, perhaps excessively devoted. The *Goodes World Atlas,* especially the thirteenth edition (1970), which I happen to find comfortable, provided most of the geography needed for the writing.[2] It cannot be copied here directly for reasons of copyright. Catherine Griffiths found alternative resources to complement the text; I'm especially pleased with the eloquent topography she found. The whole memoir would not have been possible without her assistance on matters graphic. I use the maps as necessary context, but also as decoration and congenial accompaniment; sometimes they're repeated where the terrain is complex.

A diary

Here's yours truly on a summer work trip somewhere in British Columbia not long before departure for Europe. The diary was already there, as was the diligence and the mackinaw.

The time in Europe left me with a scribble of about six hundred pages. It had helped me to metabolize places, landscapes, a magnificent array of fine art and architecture, as well as many agreeable encounters – an inner journey paralleling the outer journey.

The diary had long been difficult for me to read. I dipped into it in the 1980s when I was working on accounts of travelers into Mexico in the early nineteenth century.[3] I had come on an incisive account left by a young German who was about my age when he crossed the Atlantic. On impulse I sought out my own diary for comparison and was disappointed; it seemed shallow in its observations, full of clichés and what was least palatable, it was permeated by what struck me as exaggerated religiosity. The sceptic was embarrassed by the zealot. I didn't come back to the diary for many years.

Once the imagery of 1954–55 had become interesting in 2008–09 I began reading the diary for times and places, for explanations. It would typically take several tries before I could slide over the religiosity and keep the prose down, gradually I went from resistance to curiosity and then to a fairly determined exploration of what the young Canadian abroad had actually seen and thought.

During the early readings I did not find much *savoir faire*, not much social agility, but later, when I considered the many friends I did make and the way people were ready to show me kindness, I seemed to have done fairly well. In fact, the account of the year could have been framed as a reflection on friendship. There were stretches of solitude and loneliness too – the foreign student at a loss – but these were not obtrusive. Oh, and in the diary I had also tried to make sense of my encounters with women, all decidedly chaste.

Quick verbal sketches are the diary's most flavourful parts. A farmer and his son, for example, harness horses in their yard on a crisp winter morning, breath rising from the horses and the men. On other days, a scent of hay surrounds me on my moped. I'm frustrated by three flats in succession on the same tire before I find the tiny nail that caused them all. Anger flashes here and there. I'm not yet to the point of swearing frankly, but I'm getting there. This helped to redeem the pious young man in the eyes of the weathered octogenarian.

It became apparent that the godly talk so abundant in the diary need not be taken literally but rather as a code. The precepts and feelings could be expressed in other terms. The young man was a committed member of a Mennonite Brethren congregation and belonged, with a will, to Inter-Varsity Christian Fellowship (VCF) on the UBC campus. His motivation was lofty, he meant to realize spiritual ideals. The eighty-something in his study could certainly appreciate the young man's single-mindedness and diligence, he learned to hold back on the deprecation of naiveté. The religiosity itself became intriguing, as I'll develop here and there within the text. And, there was, in

fact, evidence of some close observation, some intellectual development, even the beginnings of a professional direction, as I've said, and gradually some refinement.

The change in my attitude toward my diary really hinged on the evidence in it of a freedom from care. By "trusting Him to supply my needs" (bits of the diary will be dropped into the account at intervals, in quotation marks, without further attribution) I could override the hassles of travel, visit museums and annotate art works, sing aloud from an open train window, while not knowing how I would get money for food and a bed in the following days. This definitely gave an edge to my exploratory travel. Later, when my inner parameters changed, it was necessary to find equanimity in other ways, fortunately the inclination toward exploratory travel remained.[4]

Early on Alice, always my first reader and unfailing supporter, encouraged me to reduce my judgement and attempt understanding. At the time I was writing the diary she was getting to like the young man and would eventually marry him, so she had a stake now in my representation of him.

Additional materials

The detritus from that first trip to Europe, the black and white positive prints accumulated somehow, the news clippings, picture postcards from museum exhibitions one was not allowed to photograph, neat little guides one could annotate and carry away, concert tickets, even menus, all this had been shaken down through successive household downsizings into a box marked ponderously: 'Memorabilia'. Many such items, plus images for which I was able to obtain explicit permission to republish, as well as others from the public domain of the web and corrective facts from reference materials, whatever enhanced or brought agreeable associations was woven into the account.

In my cache there were several consequential letters from friends. Wolfram Kretchmar, a student at the University of Hamburg who had been an exchange student at UBC in 1953–54, had many helpful suggestions for my acclimatization. Ed Hintz, friend of my youth and roommate for a time at UBC, reported to me from the home front.

My mother kept the letters I wrote home. My parents will have had a hard time reading them. I wanted to buy a typewriter while in Germany but I didn't think I could afford it. I should have sacrificed to do it. I can read the letters now, but only just, and I find what's in them difficult to keep down. The affection was genuine, but the tone is precious, preachy, very much that of the spiritually authoritative young male that I had been given to understand I was, playing to my parents' insecurities. I was doing a sales job, particularly after their automobile accident in November of 1954, convincing them and myself that it was worthwhile for me to remain abroad. These letters are thus not as candid as the diary; I have given them scant consideration.

Memory

Throughout this tracing out of a good year I have not only been gratified, or chagrined, by recollections but also repeatedly intrigued by the process of recollection. It's useful to remind oneself of how contingent and erratic it can be; that seasons the stew.

Fred Schwartzman, one of the readers of the penultimate version of this manuscript travelled with me for a time in Greece; he remembered our common experiences more or less as I did, certainly enough to sustain several long and most agreeable telephone conversations, but his details varied. Some events of the year I recalled very clearly but did not find them described in my diary and, conversely, the diary was clear about some events and some people that I couldn't remember. As I fingered transparencies I realized I was often recalling comments I had made about them after my return; these comments, regardless of their basis, had themselves become constitutive of memory. I was repeatedly pleased to watch a memory blossom after a mere indication in an image or an entry.

For someone straying wilfully into 'alien corn', that is away from straightforwardly explanatory and neatly publishable exposition, it was irresistible to match my memoirization – a rare, useful word, spellcheck be damned – against some of the published commentary on memory. Much of the recent thinking on the subject is gathered up in an essay by the neurologist Oliver Sacks. Remembering can be thought of as recreating or re-categorization, he maintains at one point. Also: "Subjectivity is built into the very nature of memory, and follows from its basis and mechanisms in the human brain."[5] Makes one feel easier.

And more: Gregory Cowles, a seasoned reviewer of memoirs, sums up a basic paradox neatly: " Even nonfraudulent memoirs, by scrupulous writers making good-faith efforts to reconstruct their pasts, are by nature unreliable – as tenuous and conditional and riddled with honest error as memory itself. And done right, that's exactly what makes them so thrilling... All memoirs are lies, even those that tell the truth... Every act of memory is to some degree an act of imagination."[6]

Early studies at UBC

The year abroad was to be part of an academic exchange, nothing terribly formal, I was given to understand, with exploratory travel alongside, but intellectually engaged nonetheless, at least that was how I took it. I would find myself near the end of the adventure deliberately taking stock of what had been exchanged. It is logical here, therefore, to ask what I brought to the experience.

I considered myself in the 'liberal arts'. As the traditional and quite lofty explanations have it; such study is meant to produce a knowledgeable and articulate, perhaps even a virtuous person. For me that meant courses in art, languages and literature, history and geography, plus as much science as I could handle – whatever promised to enlarge.

There was always a part-time job so I had my own walking around money, and there were always summer jobs, so I had my tuition and maintenance too. There was no great worry over how one would make a living eventually; times were good, there would surely be something there later.

During the first two years at UBC, I seem to have left disturbing questions in abeyance. It's ironic, since the university is notorious as a place where people can easily lose their faith, that I had my Christian spirituality immensely enhanced. I had my church and the warm supportive circle of friends in VCF. For me the chilly winds would begin to blow later. I remember that when I went for my books during the first week of the first term I opened the cover of an Anthropology text and realized immediately that here was the evolutionary view of humanity, this was some of what we had been warned about and closed the book. I wouldn't get to study Anthropology and face the whole bolus of worry about religion, missionaries, human origins, which might easily have overshadowed my undergraduate work, until I took Anthropology as a minor for my PhD.

The coat of arms of the University of British Columbia moves me still, which sounds sappy, but it does. I like the design and the dignified colours. We sewed it on our sweaters and I was pleased later to have it at the head of the stationery I had access to when I began instructing in the Geography Department at UBC in 1962.

My university seemed rich with possibilities. I have always recalled my undergraduate years as enjoyable and was amazed when my students or even our children would go down at the mouth about their undergraduate years.

Green Mackinaw

There was a special wonder about the library. For my first two years at UBC, I had a part-time job in the library as one of the retrieval persons. Borrowers asked for books on little forms at the front desk; we went down to get them. There would be no general access to the library stacks for some years yet. I remember looking down the aisles of the stacks with satisfaction. Here was the whole world. There was a special cage too, for which there was a special key that the head librarian kept about her somewhere. It was for salacious materials, including anthropological monographs about subjects like the sex life of savages. Only scholars actually doing research on such subjects could get their hands on these books, and the flunkies who searched them out and dawdled a little in the errand.

These are my fellow students in an introductory English Survey course, their faces are still vaguely familiar. We're in front of one of the surplus huts brought from an army base to temporarily accommodate a rapidly growing student body after WWII. This is how we dressed, and carried about our notes and our huge text; my

10

Alfred H. Siemens

bescribbled copy has always been within easy reach, as it is now. The Romantic Period seems to have been especially absorbing.

Some of the instruction of my first two undergraduate years turned out to be particularly good preparation for the year in Europe. Prof. Soward lectured to us from behind a barricade of books, which he would quote at intervals, going on about twentieth century world political history. This material would serve me very well as background for what I would see of the effects of recent conflicts in Europe. One of us found out that his lectures were fairly straight from a book of his own, which he had not mentioned to us. We obtained a copy and aced the course. I recognize now that I was not only at home in the VCF clubhouse but was also fortunate to be part of a loose coterie of conspirators, mostly Mennonite, who traded advice and information on professors and courses.

When a reporter in Vancouver asked me, before I left in 1954, what I proposed to study in Hamburg I said Human Geography and it got printed in *The Province*. I had only a vague idea of what this was, I had realized that it dealt with the relationship of people to their environment and this fascinated me, as it would for the rest of my life. I credit one of my undergraduate geography professors at UBC, Richard Ruggles, for making me aware of the phenomenon. His course on Settlement Geography was often excruciatingly dull, but some key ideas attracted me nevertheless. He also eventually supported the notion of a thesis on the Mennonites in the Fraser Valley and thus put me on my way to an M.A. in Geography. Prof Brünger in the Geographical Institute in Hamburg reinforced all this. During my year in Europe, I reveled in landscapes, settlement forms and the historical process of settlement in long occupied places.

Some preparation in language was obviously important. German-speaking friends and I tended to take courses in German for easy credits; occasionally we were surprised. In a course on German Literature I was introduced to Thomas Mann, particularly his novel, *Tonio Kroeger*. Serious class discussions of creativity ensued.

Our parents, immigrants from Russia in the 1920s, had worked hard to achieve a working knowledge of English, in line with the ideal of assimilation, but they also maintained the common Mennonite ambidexterity regarding German. They and their adult relatives and friends conversed in Low German, to the children they spoke High German, fairly good High German too, as in Luther's version of the bible. This was reinforced by the High German we used in the private high school, the Mennonite Educational Institute. We spoke English to our cousins and friends, but we overheard Low German. I remember listening in a corner as adults 'visited' in noisy, vivid Low German, which resurfaced remarkably in my middle age, was reinforced by such published literature and recordings as I could find to become one of the favourite diversions of my later years. In church, of course, during my early years, all was High German, then gradually English replaced it. Now I am hard put to find even among my contemporaries anyone who is prepared to venture a sentence in High or Low German, and it bothers me. I have become an oldster who bemoans the loss of language.

When I arrived in Germany I found I had a good basis on which to build fluency. My vocabulary, although fairly good in religious and literary elements, was inadequate for what I needed in university lectures and on the street. I was surprised to hear snatches of a Low German different from the one I knew, evidently there were many all over Germany. In Hamburg, I also soon detected a particular way of pronouncing High German; I didn't try to adopt that. Expletives were a revelation. In all, I gained a deliberate High German with idioms thrown in and permanently differentiated my way of speaking from the German spoken at home. When I got back my mother noticed immediately. '*Jung du sprichst night mehr so wie vorher!*' (Son, you don't speak German the way you used to.) Just as well, it occurs to me now. I hadn't been terribly fluent before Hamburg, Anglicisms had crept in and my pronunciation was flat. In this and other respects the year abroad worked well.

Of all my undergraduate studies before departure B.C. Binning's course on the history of art was most important for my European adventure.[7] We knew he was eminent, of course, and appreciated his iconic paintings and drawings. He had an intimacy with the world's art in European collections that I would go on to test and appropriate; he had clear formulations on the flowerings of styles and of important influences sweeping back and forth. He used two projectors and screens at once; I would eventually try that in my own lectures. He was at once both fascinating and approachable.

We all handed in scrapbooks of the best imagery we could find to illustrate periods and media; it was an early exercise in the laying down of pleasing pages. I happened to be working part-time in the library, as I've said, and found a morgue of disposable LIFE magazines in a sub-basement. From this cache I was able to amply illustrate it all and get a first in the course. The year in Europe allowed me the satisfaction of seeing the great art that I had pored over actually before me, in abundance. I would always maintain that this was one instance in my life when reality lived up to my expectations.

FRIDAY, SEPTEMBER 24, 1954

Departure

The journey began on a milk crate tipped into the aisle of a bus headed east out of Abbotsford. There were no seats available just then, but by Chilliwack I had a seat and a congenial travel companion too. I planned to inch my way by bus across the map of North America to Quebec City, to explore en route, visit relatives and friends, then cross the Atlantic on the *R.M.S. Franconia* to Liverpool and in early October make my way to Hamburg.

After two years at the University of British Columbia, I had received an exchange scholarship to the University of Hamburg, providing funds to study several semesters and travel during the holidays.

Additional money

The scholarship provided accommodation, maintenance and fees, plus time free to travel. During the summer of 1954 I hustled to put together the money I would need for transportation to Hamburg and within Europe as well as for additional expenses. It would be my second summer working as a dining car waiter on the Canadian Pacific Railway. You got a salary, but you also got tips and there were tricks you learned to maximize them. A table was often occupied by more than one party at a time. You exposed the good tips left on the table to other passengers and hid the meager ones. At the end of each run I would go to the nearest bank and pour out my quite presentable pyramid of coins; I could live on my tips during the summer and bank my salary.

A brief on-line search got me this visual surprise.[8] All is familiar: the room itself and the lights, the dishes and tableware we carried in and out, and polished too, the uniforms, the stances, the looks of the well-heeled travellers – this was First Class service – and the ominous presence of an almost certainly dictatorial steward. A fellow waiter on one of the cars I worked, a 'limey', briefed me on London, and I would find that very useful. Later, this summer work on the railway and other stints, in a mine, on grain farms, in orchards, doing whatever came to hand, would be fuel for boasting. This is how we made our way.

My normal run was Vancouver to Winnipeg, so I regularly passed through the farmlands of Namaka, east of Calgary, where my family had lived from 1938–1944. I seem to be off on a tangent, more like a film dissolve. There will be many more.

The main CPR line ran just off to the left of the Siemens farmstead; the gentle hill in the distance belonged to the Siksika (Blackfoot) nation; the Bow River valley was some miles to the right. The farm was part of a sparse Mennonite community. Its name, Namaka, is that of a Hawaiian sea-goddess; that luscious tropical association was probably applied here on the Albertan prairie in recognition of the Polynesians who were brought in to help build the railway.

The farm does not look forlorn to me. I know my parents invested dreams in it and hard work, it is where the preadolescent began to scan horizons, to think distance. When the young man, years later, would come by in a dining car during the summers of work on the railway, the train at full throttle, it was always meal-time and a full house, all the waiters hurrying back and forth with huge oblong trays. Sometimes I could just catch sight of the preceding landmarks and delay what I was serving enough to scan the landscape southward. During my first summer on the rails, in 1953, I saw that just the farm's granary remained, already leaning. Next summer it was gone.

We worked fifteen-hour shifts for four days and then had about that much time off at home. During these layovers I painted houses, under my own contracts or for a commercial painter, a genial Finn. Coming home after a day of painting, clean-up always took a while; mother joked for years about how she had scraped paint out of my ears so I could go out of an evening.

Crossing my country

I might be leaving on a milk crate in an aisle, but I had a booking for the *Franconia* out of Quebec City in my wallet, I was able to get up off the crate at Chilliwack and into a seat next to Henry Esau, cousin on my mother's side. He was off to the Mennonite Brethren Bible College in Winnipeg (MBBC). I remember a long conversation; at that time we shared a devoutly Christian view of the world. Night fell in the mountains, conifers moved in and out of the bus's headlights, fitful sleep.

In Calgary, another cousin, another Henry, as in Siemens, had kindly driven a long distance to fetch me to Gem, Alberta, for a brief visit to the relatives on my father's side. He has been a favourite cousin since we were kids and played nude in their irrigation ditch, exchanging what we knew of the facts of life. When my family visited Gem, on one occasion, I brought him an envelope with the parts of my wristwatch, which I had disassembled but couldn't put back together. By lunch he handed me the watch, running. I had been presumptuous in announcing myself, crossing Canada on my way to Europe, coming in like a comet and expecting a warm reception in the Siemens home. I sensed tensions within the family and clearly understood that my uncle, whose name was Henry as well, had sombre Mennonite doubts about my European adventure.

Alfred H. Siemens

There were very good friends at the MBBC in Winnipeg. The college had been one of my early options, others included a seminary in California and then there was UBC. My father helped me decide on the last of these, for which I have always been grateful. The visit to MBBC was thus an intriguing look at what might have been. When I was presented to the president, the Rev. H. H. Janzen, I was asked what I was going to study in Germany. Geography? Good, as long as I didn't study theology! I deduced that the reverend knew little of geography but that he considered theology as taught in Germany dangerous; it was liberal. I had to sample it in Hamburg, of course, and came to know something of what he meant.

My route toward Southern Ontario looped down to Chicago; it must have promised to be more interesting than a long trip around the largely unsettled northern margin of the lakes. Chicago was mainly a night of waiting in a new bus station, poking my head out just before morning, sensing danger in that grubby part of town. Ten years later I would get to read Carl Sandburg's poetry and Upton Sinclair's fiction. I came to appreciate, beyond that grubbiness, the rambunctious growth and pugnacious spirit of this city for my book, *The Americas: A Comparative Introduction to Geography* (1977).[9] I juxtaposed Chicago and Sao Paulo, as well as the central valleys of California and Chile, plus various other sets of places in the Americas in order to introduce some basics of Geography and Latin America. This worked well as a teaching device, I tested it repeatedly, but the book needed time to penetrate the more conventional array of competing texts; before long the publishers felt they had to rationalize their list and dropped my title.

It's fall here outside of my window in North Vancouver while I write of my crossing of Canada in the fall of 1954. All the seasons would go by repeatedly before this re-appreciation would be finished.

In the diary entry on fall colour in Ontario I went all symphonic, using what little I knew of musical notation: "ff- scarlet, f- red, p- orange, pp- yellow; woodwinds mellow and shaded as cider, trumpet sounds: the symmetrical deep green pines. "I took some fairly good colour transparencies as well; they were often used in my lectures, but then they vanished, perhaps lent out to one colleague or another (Siemens can illustrate anything!), more likely just fatally misfiled.

Part doggedness, part enthusiasm, it was on to Toronto, Montreal and then Quebec City. I remember being pleased to get what seemed an introduction to Europe in my own country as I went eastward. I liked to think then, and still do, that it is fortunate that my country encompasses such an intriguing province as Quebec; I acquired what seemed an obligatory token, a beret. Wandering over the Plains of Abraham, the old battlefield, I was "thrilled, I pulled up the collar of my trusty old Mackinaw. God had dealt generously with me." This was basic to my adventure. Here in the 21st century I would become intrigued by the working out of the young man's spirituality, and the beginnings of its erosion.

My one-funnel Cunard ship, the Franconia – made into a grand liner by promotional material – was waiting down at the docks below the bluff, facing westward. On the day of boarding I was about to go through customs when I realized I had left my camera in the hotel room; I had to dash back and forth in a taxi, and got back into line only just in time. It's the sort of forgetful thing I have done all my life.

On the dock, one person, a tall dark Uruguayan whom I had befriended in the city the night before, waved me goodbye. The ship turned about to face east, tea was served on deck, the Chateau Frontenac passed by on the left just up there above us,[10] a Canadian Pacific icon to thrill the Canadian Pacific dining car waiter: we were headed for the Atlantic.

Alfred H. Siemens

A modest ship with a colourful history

The Franconia had transported troops, refugees and prisoners of war, she had been Churchill's headquarters during the meeting of the Allies at Yalta in 1945. Before that she had been painted white and served as a cruisewhip into exotic ports. Her

record tells of a collision in Shanghai in 1929; she went aground off the Ile d'Orléans in the Saint Lawrence in 1950, which I'm glad I didn't know when we left by that same route. You could see her fittings had in fact been been painted often, though they looked quite sprightly to me still in 1954. I had chosen a Cunard liner deliberately to get a taste of that old way of crossing the Atlantic. I flew back from Europe in 1955, the ship was scrapped in 1956.

On the Franconia life was lazy compared to the hustle of my money-grubbing summer. There was time to meet and converse. "[I]have been able to look down

19

many another vista as this and that person talked of his plans in life, revealed his mentality." Friendship would become the descant to this trip and indeed my whole life.

The inveterate romantic walked the deck, admired the light and dark of the sea, with or without a moon, endlessly pondered the waves and sensed the air. I did my laundry and ate well. It was a pleasure to be served and not to have to serve. A brusque instructor in the gym threw me weighted balls. The sea was calm for October, except for swells; I was able to fight off seasickness with ginger ale at the bar or staying horizontal in bed.

There was also this very pleasant nurse. I showed her how to use her new 35mm camera and went with her to the 'cinema'. The movie was not affecting, but the company was. We got to the very verge of intimacy, extremely desirable but unthinkable for me. I went out on deck later, "Furious. I had an orange with me. I tore the peelings off and flung them into the sea. I consumed the rest voraciously, spitting out what I could not chew. All the while I stomped about and growled. It seemed so horrible that here again I had been snared into a perfectly painful situation by a female and my own inclinations."

Here's the fevered wrestle with the big urge. I was furious, not for having been rejected but for failing to have remained detached. It makes the octogenarian want to say, "You poor shmuck". You needed to deal with the delicacies of relating to women, wondering always about the big 'L', sublimating sex, knowing full well that any satisfaction was some distance into the future, you were mindful of the injunctions of the religious direction you had chosen; this was what it cost. Such repression was probably injurious psychologically, but it also kept the young man out of entanglements during the year abroad, and indeed until he was married in 1960. And, in addition, one constantly needed to try to sense God's will. Eventually, it would become apparent that this was illusory, worse, it was superstitious. I remember reflecting at various times during my youth on the possibility of celibacy, on monasticism, but not terribly seriously. Mennonites didn't do monkishness! Aside from that I couldn't imagine I would be able to maintain celibacy.

Land came in sight, to the south the Irish coast, the Giant's Causeway, to the north, spot lit Scottish Islands, coloured just right in heathery tones. Immediately I was scribbling and imaging landscapes, there would be great material between the North Atlantic and the Mediterranean. That inclination, strengthened and made into a habit, would be one of the most important yields of the year abroad.

The diary says that here was the, "hedged countryside I'd read so much about. Neat little green fields, properly bounded, little white specks – sheep, villages in the coves down by the seaside, and even castles … mist along the shores and clouds overhead, crowning the aged rounded mountains in the distance, the famous Grampians with Ben Lomond and all the other peaks."

Coming into the Firth of Clyde we took on a pilot, soon forms had to be filled out, then bustling and clanking. A tender took some of the passengers off at Greenock, including the nurses who were to hone their skills at a hospital in Glasgow. The ship's horn sounded, flowers were thrown and we all waved.

THURSDAY, OCTOBER 14: ENGLAND

Anglophilia

The Franconia moved south through the Irish Sea toward Liverpool,[11] past wrecks of victims of Nazi U-boats, through mists out of which cranes resolved and then long rooflines fringed by chimney pots, which I would always associate with this coming ashore. I developed a considerable liking for Brits and Britain: Anglophilia. It lasted for years, I acquired several English cars and many English friends but then eventually the affinity dimmed.

From here on I will be using a series of green maps. They're wrinkled with some fairly fascinating topography if one stares at them long enough. The places that affected me are spelled out in black, those that are used as context have been left in white. I've used the political boundaries of 1954–55 and once on the continent emphasize the barrier that would cut through Germany from the end of the war to 1989.

Liverpool was incredibly grimy. I had no reason to linger and set off with what now seem rapid moves through two weeks of England: first a taxi, and a backward look at the Franconia at dockside, much less grand than in its publicity, then by trains and buses, through a whirl of new places and acquaintances.

Young people in the first train compartment noisily introduced me to the curiosities of a Midland accent and 'Brum' the nickname for Birmingham, where we were headed on this first leg. English accents now exasperate me, I bark at the TV but watch reruns of English sitcoms and the BBC News anyway.

Spiritual considerations suffuse the diary for my two weeks in England. It may seem reductive now to emphasize the pragmatic, the educational and the aes-

Alfred H. Siemens

One had to begin with Stratford-upon-Avon, a touristic cliché if ever there was one, but first sightings can be highly satisfying. They are necessary, they are a personal appropriation. Never mind that countless others have done something like it for themselves. Enthusiasm and sensitivity, combined with some preparatory material and of course good company, light up the scenes. Before I was far into 1954–55 I would be disgusted with the casual, obviously uninformed tourism and photography going on around me. I often told my students later that I intended to spoil them for superficial travel.

Two new Aussie friends and I appropriated a good bit of Shakespeareana together. One of them caught me in what she considered a Gregory Peck pose outside of Anne Hathaway's cottage and sent me the picture later. We three booked into an old-worldly hotel, ate in a mediocre restaurant up a crooked street – all of it as if made to order for impressionable colonials and of course I believed it really had been beneficently arranged for me.

I had asked our high school literature teacher, Miss Krahn, why we had to study *Twelfth Night*. Wandering through the theatre gardens among the statures of the famous characters, the recollection of that question was an embarrassment. I was gratified to be the first of that high school class to be here. *Midsummer Night's Dream* was on the bill that night. Well, the acting, the comedy, the staging! I fell prey to enthusiasm as I wrote about it that night. I remain susceptible to such attacks.

One of the two Aussie friends went her own way, the other came with me to Oxford. We were riding top and front on a double-decker bus; we could look over hedges and walls, into the detail of village life, out onto fields and woods beyond. We would stop off and wander through the streets of some town then get back on. I was for London and Victoria Station, I don't remember where she went.

Many travel companions appear in the pages of the diary and then disappear again. Sometimes a letter or a postcard would come later, mostly not. I met a group of guys from down under who had bought a London taxi and were determined to drive it as far east as the Himalayas, as I've already said. I never heard if they made it.

in London was the home of gracious Dr. Fairbairn, of Plymouth Brethren pe... ...n and a VCF contact. I observed wh... ...emed a fine family life and marriage; I w... ...ed that. During my stay at their house, ...ed on new clothes I had bought on Oxfo.d Street: a Harris Tweed coat, wool charcoal grey pants, a collarless shirt with studs, a separate collar and French cuffs. I'd bought souvenir cufflinks on board ship. Quite a hassle to get it all together and produce the dude that

pulpits myself, just enough to know how seductive they can be.

So there I was, after a Dr. Martyn Lloyd – Jones performance. "How solid, real and solemn were his thoughts." But I was in a fix, my English money had run out and on a Sunday no one would exchange my American dollars; I could ride nowhere, I did not even have the right coins for the telephone. Not enough foresight, of course, but emphasis on *important* things and trust that the Lord would provide. Evidently, He did. It made a wonderful anecdote for subsequent devotional talks.

An immaculate Londoner in a bowler hat, very 'city' and all, saw me there in front of Westminster Chapel, obviously clueless. I liked his hat; when I began to travel in Andean South America in 1965 I found it had been carried across the Atlantic early in the twentieth century and adopted by indigenous women. The Londoner offered very graciously to help. Practical matters were soon taken care of, we fell into very agreeable conversation and a companionable walk through the London of long familiar names: Westminster Abbey, Whitehall, the Mall in the distance, Buckingham Palace, 10 Downing Street. My rescuer was Enrico de Pierro, an architect. I see now that he must have been gay; one did not resolve this issue so clearly at the time, one certainly didn't make it explicit. He had grown up in Montreal, had taught at McGill, also at UBC. He prepared a lovely lunch at his tasteful flat, all the while we talked of all manner of civilized things. A lady friend with a car then took us on a mad tour of all of London in one afternoon. There are pages of terse jiggly notes; I remember mostly the Norman (Romanesque) church of St. Bartholomew. I would warm to that style wherever I encountered it on the continent, particularly later in Spain, and I carried away a practical lesson for all those many excursions I would run later in my life: too much detail leaves a blur.

Beavering

The new arrival at the centre of all things British was diligent, very diligent; it's tiring just to read about it. This was in large part curiosity but also compensation for the modest view I had of my preparation thus far and indeed my capabilities; I needed to hustle.

In Oxford I got a strong first taste of anthropology at the Pitt Rivers Collection within the Oxford University Museum.[13] Visits to many other great museums and galleries would follow, on this journey and through the rest of my life, as well as not a little reflection on the discipline of museology, its history, its evolution. The Pitt Rivers Collection emphasized material culture, profuse and closely spaced in traditional display cases – it was put in place late in the nineteenth century. Most interesting to me in that first involvement, I don't know why, were the shrunken heads prepared by South American head-hunters. And the building must have been early in the use of structural steel, a vaguely Gothic style predominated, with Romanesque and Byzantine elements added – I was flexing my observational muscles.

Alfred H. Siemens

In the Ashmolean Museum, also in Oxford, I found more, rooms upon rooms of periods and cultures, I filled pages and pages with notes. Marvelous. At the Ashmolean I was particularly impressed by aerial photos of contemporary agriculture in various locations within the British Isles with prehistoric field patterning showing through, as on the neighbouring image, which I found later in a publication.[14] It was a seed that would sprout and grow into a strong research interest.[15]

Eventually, I did extensive aerial reconnaissance over the lowlands around the Gulf of Mexico. I was never a pilot, always an observer and photographer as well as navigator and flight director through my headphones, rather like Robert Duvall in *Apocalypse Now*. There were some genuine discoveries regarding Pre-Hispanic transportation and agriculture in wetlands by means of canals and planting platforms. A particularly clear example of *patterned ground* can be seen departing in a southeasterly direction from the airport of Veracruz, Mexico. It has always seemed to me as earth art, as calligraphy. This complex was eventually studied scientifically by Maija Heimo – to very good effect.[16]

One had to go to the British Museum. While looking at documents the wish crossed my mind that Mr. Abram Wieler, my Bible School teacher, was there with me, "It would have done him so much good." This was not a snide remark; I liked him and I knew he would have appreciated what I was seeing.

Here comes an irresistible tangent. During the winters of 1949–50 and 1951–52, I had attended The Mennonite Brethren Bible School (MBBS), where Wieler taught. A Mennonite friend asked me while I was studying there what one could possibly gain from their program. I've rethought that myself here at my computer. I didn't plan to become a minister; I did mean to be a layman with a secular profession *and* a vital Christian faith, which, it was clear to me then, needed a firm grounding in scriptural studies. However, an overriding and sufficient vindication emanates from an image that appeared in the school's annual in 1950.

Staff of the 1950 "TORCH"
ERNA ENNS; ALFRED SIEMENS; ABE KLASSEN; TILLY BORN; JOHN KRAHN
MR. A. WIELER (Faculty Sponsor); JACOB SUDERMAN (Ed.-in-chief)
KATHRYNE MATTHIES

It's a pleasure to see these people again and remember the conviviality at MBBS, then in its first home in South Abbotsford. We took curious courses about cults and the symbolism of Jewish holy places. There was something called homiletics, the art of preaching. I remember my trial sermon and could probably give it again now. Rev. Wieler sat in the back row and couldn't keep a straight face. There was nothing systematically philosophical or theological in the teaching, at least nothing that stuck with me. We certainly gained a familiarity with the Bible. Passages out of the Luther or King James versions, which respectively dominated the two language realms of our lives, come to mind freely to this day. They would surface, alternating with Grandmother Wiens' Low German sayings, as completely appropriate but hardly directly usable formulations during my decidedly secular lectures at the university.

I went to the British Museum several times and was finally pretty much overwhelmed. I would need to take courage, there were many more museums to come.

Red flowers bordered the black tombstone of David Livingstone on the floor of Westminster Abbey. *"Born by faithful hands over land and sea ..."* is how the famous inscription begins. I was impressed, as well, by the memorial window for the flyers of the Battle of Britain in the Lady Chapel of Westminster Abbey.[17] The kid in Namaka, on the Prairies, listening to the table radio shaped like a gothic arch heard bombs falling on London.

While in London I got my first letter from home, it was a thrill, but I noted that I was very absorbed by my new environment and felt no homesickness. There was too much to see and do.

Oxbridge pilgrimages

During my undergraduate days at UBC Inter-Varsity Christian Fellowship (IVCF or just VCF) was more important to me than my studies or my church. The club had elected me president for the 1953–54 academic year, and would do so again in 55–56. I felt out of my depth much of the time, sustained and helped out of scrapes, I believed, only by God's grace, which makes for great inspirational talking points. "Seek ye first the kingdom of God and his righteousness and all these things shall be added on to you." That's how St. Matthew has it (6:33). Put spirituality first and studies will somehow be facilitated. It had to be possible to maintain a Christian life in an intellectual environment.

The octogenarian can still hear the young man sweep an audience with exhortation, energize a committee, preach and pray. He received an award for campus leadership; he would always look back on having had a satisfying level of influence during that VCF time. There would never be anything quite like it again.

Alfred H. Siemens

VCF had roots in Oxford and Cambridge; I needed to make special visits out of London to related club facilities in both in order to get whiffs of that background to which we on the UBC campus were often referred. There's a good description of VCF in the UBC yearbook.[18] We had "amazing habits" our fellow students said, we met often in our clubhouse in Hut B-4, and indeed conducted informal bible study once a week and then more bible study still in a private home on Sunday afternoon. We were serious, and yet joyful, they thought, and they were quite right; our clubhouse was a warm base, no drifting alienation on a large impersonal campus for us.

In Vancouver the VCF Sunday bible study took place at the Wright Mansion in Shaughnessy. This and another bible study that I headed at roughly the same time in the Fraserview Mennonite Brethren Church, were the two urns into which I poured my youthful spirituality, appropriating scripture and expounding it with imagination, not much coherent theology, but such interpretational and verbal skills as I could muster. The bible that I mostly used at the time heads my shelf of bibles here in my study now; its emphatic underlinings and marginal notes prompt many recollections.

I continued this fervent advocacy in presentations to a Mennonite Sunday School and youth groups in Germany. I suspect this was often considered exaggerated in those more reserved contexts. I had come to view Christian discipleship as the great brilliant objective, but also as relentlessly demanding. I've never been able to see Christianity as a comfortable refuge.

At Henry Martyn Hall, headquarters of Inter-Varsity Christian Fellowship in Cambridge, I noticed the posted prayer concerns and was stopped by this request: "Praise for eight conversions at the Halloween Party at the Technical College last night." Curious on the face of it, but not at all incredible to me then. I knew already that one could have hallowed fun at VCF parties.

The Hall impressed me as a memorial and a hearth; the floors had been worn by many feet, from here had gone famous missionaries. On the wall was a picture of David Livingstone, inscribed 'Yours affectionately'.

One should really be a Cambridge man to dare to use the iconic image of King's College. I have lifted it out of my photo collection because I remember entering, hearing an organist practising and admiring the way the sun slanted through stained glass windows and painted the floor.

The spires, quads and colleges of Oxford are spread out before any number of vantage points; in my diary I interpreted them in terms of art periods![19] High street was covered with a rubber silencer: a bit of quiet for the dons. We wheel through Oxford frequently now in one or another of the detective series imported by the Knowledge network.

"The low sun lit up some [Oxford college grounds], shaded others. Birds sang and the air was bracingly cool … I drew in great gulps of educated oxygen."

At the Oxford chapter of the equivalent of VCF I was moved in a student prayer meeting. "Fervent, vital and specific … asking for the conversion of people they knew, for opportunities of contact, establishment of new converts, for whom they thanked."

The geographer Jim Houston was then at Oxford; somehow I came to eat porridge at breakfast in his house and to chat about the new post-war British work in oblique air photography of which I had seen examples at the Ashmolean. He also lent me his bike. I heard him lecture about God and nature in Old Testament times, God working through nature, using nature, to miraculous effect. This was important to me because I intended to become a Christian academic, to advance my spiritual life and that of others by maintaining my faith *and* my intellectual integrity. I'm no longer interested in such apologetic gymnastics. I prefer scientific explanations of natural phenomena and an anthropological explanation of God. Ethics and environment, yes, that is supremely relevant, of course. I liked Houston, eventually he became a senior colleague in the Geography Department at UBC and then a founding principal of Regent College. He kindly donated his personal library to the Geography Department's library; I helped to integrate them.

In Hamburg I would become acquainted with a continental university system. At Oxford I caught, in passing, some ideas about still another system. They were corroborated when I met Oliver, an Oxonian, in Greece some months later, and I'll get to him in due course. At UBC soon after my return I befriended Geoffrey Hurley and Bob Price, graduate students from the UK with me in the M.A. Geography program.

This picture was easy to include; it signals an advanced stage in the Anglophilia that had begun for me before I went to England and then grew for a while afterward. Bob, on the right, is gone. Recently I googled Geoff on impulse and there he was, immediately, looking just as he does here. He was representing commercial interests, if I'm not mistaken, with a base in Hong Kong. I wanted at first to contact him, but drew back, our worlds might well be unbridgeable, there would have had to be too much explanation.

In any case, my two friends thought we worked too hard at courses, wrote too many exams and were altogether too busy. At English universities there were few lectures to attend. One had several tutorials a week: one to one meetings with a professor, for which one had written an essay, which was then discussed. There was time for an academic and a social life, to say nothing of spiritual fellowship, all of which, together with the architecture and that special oxygen, had impressed me in Oxford.

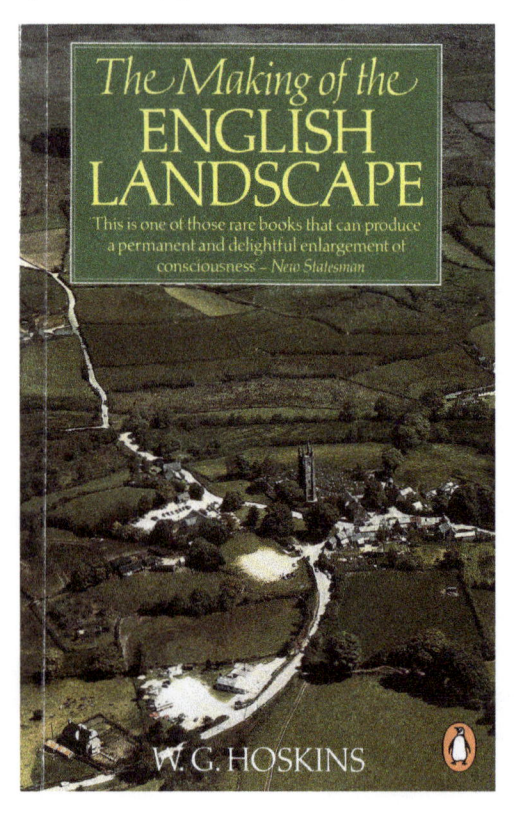

Shortly after my return to Canada my father helped me to buy an Austin A40 Devon.[20] That's one of the many things that I'm grateful to him for. In it we three would take out student nurses and then hurry them back across town to their residence before their curfew fell.

Looping south from London

Most of this was again on double-decker busses, peering over hedges and walls, catching glimpses of gentle horizons and the wonderfully cultured English landscapes, cultured in contrast to the more recently occupied and still raw landscapes of my home. I've belabored the word culture throughout my professional life and I suppose I have emphasized its material aspects, especially the structures and the marks left by people in the landscape.

Here in Southern England, houses, fences and walls, all with their respective local building materials, the bridges, plants, animals, cultivation techniques, village siting and form, the woods on the subdued hills, the geomorphology, which I was beginning to understand, all these composed themselves endlessly, turn after turn. I was enthusiastic already about the idea of *landscape* with so much more to come, and I see now that I was preparing myself for Hoskins' exemplary *The Making of the English Landscape*.[21] It was published in 1955 but I didn't find out about it until quite a few years later. When I did I inflicted it on my students repeatedly, even in Mexico. It organized formative factors and epochs, it presented a template – which had to be taken with reservations – for a consideration of the relationship of people and their environment through time, as good a formulation as any of my own lasting academic interest.

I happened into Bognor Regis, the coastal resort town just east of Southampton, on a train just after midnight. There were no more trains; as I left the depot attendants and conductors came out behind me and shut it all down. I tried a telephone booth as an overnighting possibility – not promising. I tap-tapped in my leather-soled shoes along a cobbled street when a bobby appeared at its end, waiting for me. He was kind and directed me to what he considered the only option, a high-priced hotel – far out of my youth-hosteling budget, of course, but unavoidable under the circumstances.

Great to be able to spend a good bit of one's youth deciphering cathedrals. I had looked forward to seeing the sharp spire of Salisbury's cathedral on the Salisbury Plain. The printed guide I got at the door approximated my mental image rather well. In my diary I detailed portals, the lovely cloister, integrating what I was seeing with what I had learned.

Two other places on that loop out of London come to mind: Wells, not far west of Salisbury, and Bath. The cathedral at Wells had already found its way into my paste-up project book for B.C. Binning in his nutritious course at UBC. The cathedral has this great facade, of course, with its lower row of saints knocked out by rampaging Puritan soldiers.[22] I wanted to

Alfred H. Siemens

photograph the striking inverted arch inside, but was collared by an irate verger – one who keeps order – and made to pay a fine. Hadn't I read the notice? He had obviously become disgusted by tourists and particularly by anyone from America, a term the English apply indiscriminately. Well, Mr. Verger, here's to you.[23]

In the Cathedral's chapter house, a place where clergy meet, I found this piano passage in stone.[24]

Alfred H. Siemens

Binning had gone on and on about early, that is eighteenth century, urban planning in Bath: Georgian style architecture, with formal façades and rather unsightly backs, rooms arranged vertically within units, making for cumbersome housekeeping but facilitating sweeping geometric arrangements, as in the Royal Crescent – an early realization of pleasing urban aesthetics.[25] I tramped around making the comparisons with planned interventions in city structure elsewhere in the world that we had been encouraged to think about. In the diary I concluded that, "This is a great life."

SATURDAY, OCTOBER 30: HAMBURG

'Die Freie und Hanzestadt Hamburg'

This is the official name of the city to which I had been invited: a free imperial city of the Holy Roman Empire and a member of the medieval Hanseatic league of trading cities. Wow. This would be my city until I left for the Mediterranean in February, and again when I returned from there in mid-May. It remained 'my city' for the rest of my life. I returned to it varous times in the 1960s; it became a recollection etched into a crystal ball, like those they sell you in better souvenir shops.

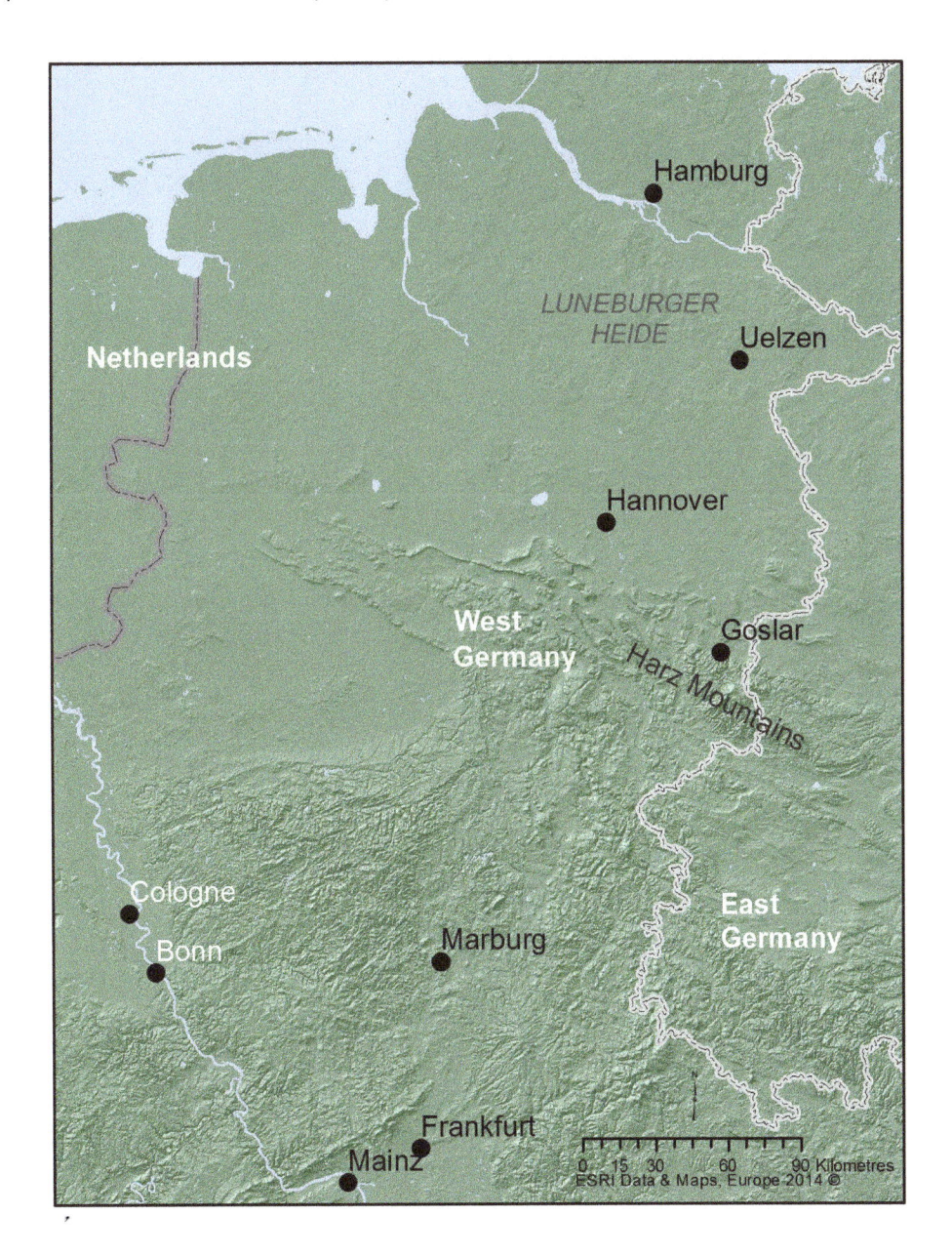

Alfred H. Siemens

My arrival late in the evening of October 30, is flavoured by the recollection of 'Teewurst', a savoury tube of pâté, quite new to me, bought at a railway station kiosk. It was all I could find to eat at that hour.

Someone answered my call to the university's office for international students' affairs, the *Akademische Auslandstelle*, and kindly directed me via the rapid transit system, the S-Bahn, through Dammtor station and on to a small suburban stop called Klein Flottbek. Nearby, at Papenkamp 16 was the house where a small upstairs room had been rented for me. It had a window on a garden, from which I would watch the seasons of 1954 and '55.

By public transit and on foot, a great deal on foot, I searched out an ambit within the central city, an array of shops, parks and restaurants that would be useful to me, a territory that would became familiar and amenable. At night the lights and spires of the centre of the city appeared velvety and dramatic to me. They were colourful and messy on the cover of a map that I picked up early on and will refer to again later. Hamburg's coat of arms is on the wallet I carried, European style, in my inner coat pocket, and which I still have.

'Hummel, Hummel'

I had come to a city with a long, colourful history, bombed heavily during the war but rebounding well, becoming an important port again and a lively centre of trade. It was a fort, a 'Burg', in the ninth century, located on the Elbe River near the sea. From the thirteenth to the seventeenth centuries it had been a member of the Hanseatic League, an economic alliance of coastal cities from the Baltic to the North Sea. Always independently inclined it had been a sovereign state in the nineteenth, a state under the Nazis, part of the postwar British Zone of Occupation after WWII and then from 1949 a part of the new Federal Republic of Germany. I was given to understand that it was still a very particular place; people here had their ways, they gave German a particular pronunciation, as I'll demonstrate in a page or two and had their own version of Low German. They were also pugnacious and might well use an old antiphonal wordplay as, say, in battle cries or at a football match. The story goes that in the nineteenth century fresh water was brought along streets in Hamburg by a water carrier whom kids would tease with 'Hummel, Hummel', a derision the origin of which is not clear. He would reply with 'Mors, Mors', that is to say, 'Kiss my ass'.

My landlady explained that Germans were not as particular as North Americans about personal hygiene, I could have one bath a week but could wash my feet every day, if I wished. I had no access to a kitchen or even a refrigerator, so I learned to eat, and eat well, combining perhaps one meal a day at a student refectory or a modest restaurant with goodies kept in a tin box of about one cubic foot that I kept under my bed. Milk sat in a carton on the windowsill. I was able to get wonderful breads, cheeses, ham and jam too, plus fruit and juice at nearby shops. I had food like this out of my knapsack when I travelled. Alice and I still often forage in local stores and eat picnic style when we are on the road. The parents sent me a package including a cake much of which was in crumbs after the trip across the Atlantic. I carefully scooped them all up.

In the package was also a bag of roasted buns, which I soaked in milk. Such roasted buns served as durable shipboard provisions for centuries. The Mennonites brought sacks of them on their voyages across the Atlantic, as did my mother's family in 1926. Alice now bakes and roasts them wonderfully, in the traditional manner. These, on our counter in North Vancouver, are like the buns that I was sent from home in 1954.

Dammtor

This is now a first exploration of the city, as Green Mackinaw began to live it; he will scan it again in June of 1955 before he leaves. Dammtor railway station: a high, curved chilly metal concourse, comes to mind. I came and went there almost every day. I immediately hear the whine of arriving and departing electric trains, feel the gusts of winter air and the cold benches. Compartment doors whack and waves of passengers hurry by. From the loudspeakers I get the first peculiarities of Hamburg German: Not *"Der Zug fährt an auf Bahnschteig zwei"* (Train arriving on platform two) but rather *"Der Zuck fährt an auf Bahnsteig zwo."* I would be intrigued to watch for this treatment of vowels and consonants, not that I intended to copy it.

Countless times after I'd settled into a seat on the commuter inter-urban out of Dammtor station, I watched the platform begin to move. The engine drivers, it seemed to me, must take great pride in the smoothness of their application of power. Eventually I would gather a bundle of such sensations, the essence of coming away. In Quebec City, when the *Franconia* was loaded and the lone Uruguayan friend in black had waved, I had watched the farewell streamers stretch and snap. Departure by air gets me in the gut, I have never tired of it, the roar as throttles are pushed forward, the release of brakes, acceleration and then the tilt. Smaller, lightly loaded jets do it best, they can make a steep ascent.

When I had become committed in my research to aerial exploration in the 1980s, I would sometimes need to substitute a helicopter for a wing-overhead propeller plane. Capitán Fernandez, of Veracruz took me up in his dragonfly, his soap bubble. I looked closely as our runners separated from the asphalt. The Capitán loved to fly and offered to show me how he kissed a pasture. It was a golden afternoon, he brought us down to just touch the grass and then revved away. Of all the various ways of leaving I have enjoyed none more than the ascent of a balloon, as one morning a few years ago over Cappadocia. When all were aboard and the globe was taut, the pilot valved up some flame, the handlers let go. I leaned over the edge so I could see the basket separate from the ground.

Back to Dammtor. It evokes not only sounds and sliding departures but foods: gritty pressed figs I could get in trackside shops and something more, the skin pop and tangy taste of hot 'Würstchen', rather like the European wieners we now buy in Vancouver, served on a long thin paper plate, with a dash of mustard and a piece of bread, and also usually a plastic cup of hot milk. I had that many times at a snack bar on the platform, with steam rising from my hot milk. I've tried to recapture these sensations on subsequent passes through German railway stations – not the same, neither the sausages nor I.

Alfred H. Siemens

In one or another of the Hamburg bookshops I found a little collection of watercolours by various artists. I would have set an endnote but the necessary bibliographical data isn't there. It includes Günter Gattermann's summery 'Jungfernstieg' ('Maiden's Walk') above. It rims the *Binnenalster*, a basin in the waterway that runs east to west into the Elbe River (There will be a map of central Hamburg later). I walked here often, joyously, open to new impressions. There were some economical restaurants nearby: I remember delicious 'Bratkartoffeln', fried potatoes, and 'Bohnensuppe', white bean soup. One could eat and drink well in the vaulted mayor's eatery, the 'Ratsweinkeller'. It's in the lower story of the 'Rathaus', or city hall – as in Siegfried Oelke's rendering. It fits under the spire on the right of the image of the Jungfernstieg.

Ground bricks and glass

Students were recognized as penurious wherever I went in Europe, and given special rates and passes. There was a kind of discount store for students in a repurposed WWII bunker near the university, you went down a stairway past walls of raw concrete. The war was still evident otherwise too. Bombed out structures not yet removed raised empty-eyed facades against the sky. Lines of buildings had had large sections blown out, leaving snaggle-tooth survivors. Between sidewalks and roadways I noticed the crushed residue of glass and bricks. Among the people on the streets there were often men missing an arm or a leg. Trees along the Alster, crookedly regrown, allowed one to imagine blasted limbs.

Later, in Mainz, I would come on an area where ruin removal was not as far along as in Hamburg. This was symbolic for me. I had heard bombs falling when I was a kid in Namaka and imagined the results. There must have been a lot of detritus of blasted homes and offices among the bricks and twisted supports. I was right and picked up a bent pair of scissors as a souvenir.

The collection of Hamburg watercolours includes one of the Ohlsdorf Cemetery by Reina Frank. Thousands of the victims of the Allied bombing in July of 1943 are buried in mass graves. There is grim photographic evidence too of the effects of a firestorm, the hellish convergence and updraft of flames over an area intensively bombed, including the incineration of this messenger who was caught

Alfred H. Siemens

in the open.[26] Out along the Elbe there were still the dynamited U-boat bunkers that had been bases for submarines that harried Allied shipping in the Atlantic.

'Wer hätte das gedacht…'

The harbour itself clattered with activity. The city was reclaiming its old function. Hamburg in 1954–55 was participating fully in the country's economic resurgence. The formidable Konrad Adenauer was West Germany's 'chancellor'. In my file of memorabilia there is this cartoon clipped early in 1955 out of the newspaper *Die Welt*; I was beginning to appreciate this paper and the magazine *Der Spiegel* too, beginning to disdain the tabloid *Bild*.

Anyway, as 1955 was rung in, the Germans themselves were amazed, a new German army was being formed. *"Wer hätte das gedacht?"* Who would have thought it, so soon after WWII? A one-page handout that I picked up somewhere identified a preoccupation of the time: Germany must be reunified, the formation of an army in West Germany, counterpoised to the army forming in the Soviet Zone (East Germany), would increase tensions between East and West and prejudice reunification.

Alfred H. Siemens

The Berlin Wall would go up in 1961 and not come down again until 1989; reunification began soon after that, but has not been fully internalized to this day. There are still places that have an East German aspect, people who are seen as and regard themselves as 'East Germans'; they're sometimes called 'Ossies', from 'Ost'.

Delicious satire was coming out of the Soviet Zone, as on the cover of this issue of *Tarantel,* (literally 'tarantula', a poisonous spider, but with who knows now what subtle overtones). Voluptuous Mother Russia, in the form of her president Georgi Malenkov, is once again taking advantage of the less than imposing leader of East Germany, Walter Ulbricht. Something like that.

'Practically lifeless and continually losing ground'

Arrival in Hamburg had been on the evening of October 30; I was surprised to find in the diary that on the very next day, a Sunday, just by looking in the telephone directory. I had found a Mennonite church but then the whole year seems fast-paced and hence longer than a year would normally be.

There was an evening service, a "Gemeindeabend", at their imposing church in the district known as Altona. Immediately ready to judge, I scribbled on the printed program that the singing was "unspirited – words good, but without feeling", the homily, "completely dead". The youth group that met afterwards, however, was attractive. I sensed among them something of the spiritual vitality I had known in VCF. They were good fun too. Soon I was participating in regular weekly meetings, teaching in a children's Sunday school they sponsored and going on a number of youth group retreats. These helped me to get to know a good bit of the north of the country, as well.

Alfred H. Siemens

Mennonites were my warmest friends in 1954–55, especially Bob Detweiler, who was in Germany under the 'PAX' program, organized by the Mennonite Central Committee (MCC) as an alternative service for American conscientious objectors to the draft.[27] He and others were constructing houses for war refugees near Wedel, just outside of Hamburg. Netty Redekop, a Canadian, had a supervisory position in that same project; she was a kind of housemother. She's there in the picture with the Sunday schoolers and the Canadian sporting his new London suit. Helmut Funke led the youth group that I attended that first Sunday. There were others: Doris Nikkel, Helmut's girlfriend, Peter Grund, Leonard Gross. With them and others, in a gutless VW van, or "combi", I was able to get out into northern Germany's countryside. Here's Helmut on the left and a friend whose name I don't remember. I very much appreciated Erwin Kornelson, a German pastor in a Mennonite church outside of Hamburg – he would eventually move to British Columbia and take up a pastor's position in a Mennonite church on the Lower Mainland.

Sundays I usually went out to the MCC community development project at Wedel, a bit beyond the end stop on one of the lines of the S-Bahn. I taught the children's Sunday school there, which I found absorbing. I even wrote to the editor of the Mennonitische Rundschau, published in Winnipeg, for Sunday school materials. In my diary I noted how things went, disconcerted when a session wouldn't take off, very pleased when it worked. I wanted them to catch some of my spiritual enthusiasm. Exaggerated piety, they may well have thought, I think it now. To and from Wedel I often walked alone: crisp rural tree-lined landscapes, and one winter's night a bright moon.

There was always lively talk, wherever we were, at the PAX headquarters in Wedel, underway in the VW to a retreat, in related visits to homes, just going to movies or even a political street rally. I recall clearly one discussion in which we addressed the question: *"Was ist ein Mennonit?"* (What is a Mennonite?) A follower of Menno Simons,[28] certainly, but beyond that we came down on the affirmation that such a person is in fact a believing Christian, a disciple of Christ, and I certainly assented. That equivalence sounds a bit presumptuous now.

In about a decade after those intense discussions I had come to think of Mennonitism in broader, cultural terms. I was happy to eat Mennonite food and participate in Mennonite folkways. My friends know me now, I think, as someone who has some capacity for and certainly a fondness of Low German, as well as a fair grasp of Mennonite History – after all I did my Master's thesis on the Mennonites of the Fraser Valley.[29] The theological strainings, however, bore me. People come up to me with emotion and recall the time when I ran a lively young people's Bible Class in the Fraserview Mennonite Brethren church, or when I soloed hymns. I am awed too, but I think of that now as another life.

Bob introduced me to Hamburg's red light district, the Reeperbahn, where the women sat in the windows, slid panels back and called to passing guys. We only looked, of course. Brightly coloured neon lights overhead advertised liquor and gambling and signalled clubs. Who knew what went on in there! All very illicit, but legal, and grubby. But I remember feeling dry in the mouth. Bob and I discussed love, liquor as well as spiritual stultification within the Mennonite community of northern Germany. He had access to an MCC-provided stock of food supplies in the Altona

Mennonite Church, such as huge cans of meat in sauce, which he would take to enrich the Spartan menus at youth retreats. There was also at least one huge cylinder of well-aged cheese, from which he eventually carved a large wedge for me to take in my knapsack on the trip to the Mediterranean in early spring of 1955.

With several PAX-boys and some others I found myself in Cologne's fine youth hostel, on the way to some event. We were awakened in the morning by the rich, lovely low notes of a cello played by our host in the stairwell. The diary doesn't mention this, but memory has held it.

The cathedral, 'der Kölner Dom', had been damaged during the war; an air photograph has preserved that dismal scene.[30] When we were there in 1954 and looked down from the spire there were still extensive ruins, many surmounted by cranes. The reconstruction seemed tasteful and reserved, as in Hamburg. Here was my first continental Gothic architecture, a continuation of the cathedraling begun in England and to be continued off and on for the rest of my life. I found a miniature of the cathedral of Cologne that I had sent my parents in their effects after they were gone.

On that same trip we went to the US army base in Frankfurt; the MCC had somehow mediated for PAX boys, and their guests an access to the 'PX', the Post Exchange, i.e. the commissary selling equipment and provisions to army personnel.

We ate hamburgers and drank Cokes, which one couldn't yet do anywhere else in the country, and went to operas on two successive nights: Bizet's *Carmen* and Wagner's *Tannhaüser*. The fiery Spanish music caused a bit of heartburn in the diary; I was convincing myself that one needn't empathize overly much with love lyrics, you certainly shouldn't take them literally. Fifty years later I had to be reminded of that again in Mexico City. This is a basic problem for me: I can't help paying attention to the words of songs; it makes it difficult for me to listen to Country and Western or Mexican "ranchera" music. I can't just let it wash over me, just as I tend to listen to what preachers actually say.

Carmen had a surrealistic cold night sequel: the Combi's battery went dead, we pushed, we walked, and we laughed helplessly. The diary has a bit of an analysis of Tannhaüser too, but what I carried away was a line of monks, dark figures moving across a minimalist stage, singing the Pilgrim Chorus.

It occurred to me here on a May morning in 2012: Where is Bob Detweiler now? I have only gradually become used to the idea over the last few years that one can find answers to most anything easily now. His picture came up immediately and I recognized him.[31] Sadly, it was part of an obituary, Bob had died in 2008. Evidently he had been a respected scholar, had written some good books, and had been an excellent teacher, a valued mentor, a joker. I remembered laughing with him, often. And then a stunner: he had "left the Mennonite faith as an adult." We would have had much more to share, had I known.

In my cache of memorabilia I found, on creased onionskin, a copy of the report that he wrote, sometime in the late 1950s on "Mennonite Youth Work in North Germany." He affirmed the significance of personal faith, as I would have done then, but with more reserve. In his report he had considered, "That the Mennonite Church in North Germany [was] already practically lifeless and continually losing ground. The youth [program] … was attempting to build an active program within the framework of a nearly dead church." I remembered my reaction to the first 'Gemeindeabend'.

Burrowing further into my cache I found a delightful letter written to me in early 1955 by Edwin Hintz, one of those blue aerograms filled to the last square centimetre with goings on at home.[32] It included mention of a report I had written in German on my experiences in Germany for the *Mennonitische Rundschau*, the key Mennonite weekly in North America.[33] I had forgotten about it. In it there is dismay regarding the Mennonite church I had found in Hamburg, similar to Bob's dismay, but that's outweighed by warm appreciation of the youth group. Apparently the report worked well, it was read aloud at an end-of-year 'Watch Night Service,' which as I remember was always a solemn, stock-taking occasion.

The wording of the report detains me now. I compare it to the other ways of speaking apparent in this memoir. It's as though I had cleared my throat and assumed circumspection. The *Rundschau* piece is in fairly good German, but then my German was strong in spiritual parlance, it needed work for the street and for academic discourse. I was conscious of the readership: church people, including such as might well be dubious of the spiritual commitment of university students and apprehensive about their influence on young people still at home – like my Uncle Henry Siemens. I was nothing if not sincere, and a bit fervent too, I'm sure, but careful to stay in context. The report was much less personal and more reserved in tone than my defensive letters home, of course, and quite different too from the confidential, frank and deeply spiritual entries in the diary. All of this, the events and encounters of a good year, are recounted in quite another parlance after the passage of many years and basic shifts in my personal terms of reference – implied only too clearly at many points, I'm sure. What a cross-echoing of voices! Hopefully not just noisy but complementary.

The gap between what pertained then and what holds now: Will I accede to urgings for an explication, a sequel to this re-appreciation of 1954–55? Will I deal with what my daughter calls the elephant in the path? Perhaps, if there is time, but I won't relish it, I don't think, like I have the preparation of this memoir. I'll probably need to resort to a geomorphological metaphor: the erosion of faith was not deliberate, it happened with the wind and the rain.

What of that Altona Mennonite Church now? I challenged my browser and up came, *"Wilkommen bei den Mennoniten in Hamburg"* (Welcome among the Mennonites in Hamburg), with updated worship and study topics, all sorts of contact information and a handsome picture of the church.[34] Who says 'lifeless' now? And what does that mean anyway?

'Wenn der Hahn kräht auf dem Mist'

I'll get to the subhead shortly. Human Geography, I'd said to the reporter in Vancouver when asked what I proposed to study. I did not yet appreciate how rich a field this was, but I had realized that it dealt with the relationship of people to their environment and that the study of this involved a careful consideration of the natural environment as well as the works of man – all varying over time. It was logical that I should gravitate toward the Geographical Institute at the University of Hamburg, which became my academic base for 1954–55.

The entrance is elegant in my photograph, lightly sepia too, and fiftyish. I spent many hours in its reading room, ironically a lot of it reading Richard Hartshorne, a noted American geographer – in English! I would have a good deal more to do with him when I began my PhD at the University of Wisconsin some five years later; he was one of our professors.

This was not one of Germany's famous old universities and the main building seemed stodgy. There had been antecedent institutions from the seventeenth century, but not a university as such until 1919. However, there were more than enough resources for me to be getting on with.

In Oxford I had already sensed that there were other ways of studying than those I knew, and English friends in our own Geography department at UBC would substantiate that. Now, in Hamburg, I was lifted from a tightly structured and sequenced system of courses in the North American manner and dropped into make-of-it-all-what-you-will. There was no program other than what I could come up with myself in discussions with friendly professors and in speculative grazing. There were no exams for anyone, it seemed, until one went for a doctorate, and then it was trial by fire, ranging over everything one had studied. I watched thoroughly harried senior students preparing for such exams and thought that our staged system of examinations had much to recommend it. Not many years later the German university system would be extensively altered too, bringing it more in line with the North American way.

My impressions were corroborated in an address by the Rektor (the president), to new students in late November. I made the following notes in my diary:

> He dwelt heavily on the great advantage of academic freedom as allowed in the German university ... the effect of this system toward broad enlightenment, toward thorough, rounded knowledge ... a greater ability to choose, to single out the important ... There were no prescribed courses, no precise system of prerequisites. For several years the student, dependent only on the prod of his own initiative, studied what he judged necessary, naturally with some measure of guidance. In the process of elimination he came in contact with many secondary issues, many ideas beyond his own particular interest, with the result: broadening. [The Rektor] deplored the trend toward successive specialization and the unnatural system of "writing off" blocks of material in frequent examinations. (I wonder if he was seeing the North American in his audience.) A final examination gave a true indication of the sum total. That, he felt, was most meaningful. He mentioned the trend here in Germany toward examinations at more frequent intervals, maintaining his favour of the older system.

The Hamburg experience reinforced a basic view of the academic enterprise already nascent while I was at UBC: it was personally motivated, free-ranging and humanistic, with scientific additives as needed. I propounded this view directly or indirectly during my teaching at UBC and in various universities in Mexico. I'm grateful that I no longer need to try to advocate it to undergraduates. It was never easy, but now with student indebtedness, poor job prospects and the generalized consideration in our society of 'academic' as a longish four-letter word, it seems unconscionable when baldly stated, but retains a strong residual value, of course.

There were many occasions in youth group meetings and at the university, as well as later on the road, when I needed to explain myself, my studies and my country. A fellow-student in the Hamburg University cafeteria sits before an 'Eintopf', a huge bowl of starchy noodles as far as I can tell, the least expensive, one-dish meal in the place. 'You come from Canada? It must be wonderful to live there.' I would hear reactions like this repeatedly throughout my time in Europe, they became a lasting part of my view of my own country: immensely attractive to prospective in-migrants, a dream, a great place to be from, and to come back to. I still think that every time I touch down at the Vancouver airport.

I will have seemed a very green undergraduate in the Hamburg University, with or without my Mackinaw, 'uncool' in the eyes of my fellow students and professors, I'm sure, although the term wasn't in use yet. Perhaps I was just an intriguing exotic. I had not yet learned much of Greece and Rome, not a great deal of the 'Classics' in my formation thus far, but I intended to work on that in spring. My German was still deficient for the street and indeed for proper academic articulation. I cringe at remembered faux pas in university seminars, but I soldiered on, little deterred, with weekend escapes into English in the company of my PAX friends at Wedel.

One of the professors at the institute offered a series of lectures on climatology just manageable for me; I never forgot his closing line: *"Wenn der Hahn kräht auf dem Mist so verändert sich das Wetter oder es bleibt wie es ist."* Loosely translated/explained: Every peasant farmyard had its pile of manure. I had seen such a manure pile on one or another of the excursions southward out of Hamburg with my Mennonite friends. It was always a sign of good farm management. If the cock perched on this pile and crowed, the professor maintained, the weather might change or it could stay the same – a fine comment on the vagaries of the air and the limits of forecasting.

This traditional farmhouse provides context for the climatologist's quip. It is itself worth a careful look, as they usually are. It offers shelter for man and beast; we see the rear entrance, for the animals. The construction is *Fachwerk* – wooden framing with brick filler. This house was built with artistic sensitivity: a slight asymmetry, a division of space as gracious as a painting by Mondrian. The bevelled gable is characteristic of the farmhouses of the Lüneburger Heide, of which I would see more. The two medallions are *hex signs,* meant to bring good luck, keep evil spirits out. German immigrants brought this notion to Pennsylvania some centuries ago. And obviously this is the northern terminus for a pair of migratory storks.

Other fare at the institute stuck to my ribs as well, such as Prof Brünger's lectures on settlement studies and the methodology of geography, Prof Ottremba's economic geography and someone's presentations on nomadism in central and eastern Asia. Elsewhere in the university I sought out some theology, some sociology, some archaeology and German agrarian history. I even tried to learn some French, from a German base: pretty hopeless. I remember the lady instructor begging us: *"Ich flehe Sie an."* Please, please practise. I didn't, but I should have. I would soon find out how limiting a lack of fluent French could be when an academic from western Canada found himself at meetings in Ottawa and Montreal.

If there was talk of a particularly good lecturer anywhere in the university, you went to the class before in the appropriate room so you would have a seat when the crowd streamed in. Thus I heard the famous theologian Thielicke, on a classical conflict situation exemplified in one of Dostoyevsky's novels: Do ends justify the means? Another lecturer compared Hegel and Kirkegaard, "but I didn't know enough about either of them to be critical. Beneficial nevertheless." Makes me smirk now, here at my computer, I wonder what I thought the benefit might be. I've already come clean to various of my friends about my philosophical deficiencies; I never became proficient enough to drop these heavy names as well as I needed to for truly sophisticated intellectual discussion. Eventually one philosopher did become important to me and I'll make room for him later.

And there were means of instant feedback in the lecture room. You whacked your palms on the desktop when you were really taken with what had been said, you pushed your shoes back and forth on the floor when you were not. Either way you could drown the professor out.

The booklet that was sent to foreign students coming to study in Germany gave me a great many clues, including right there on the cover the tantalizing extracurricular possibilities. It was not just possible but advisable, it seemed, to combine study with travel. Confirmation of what I already felt personally.

I learned something about what 'assistant professor' meant; I would get to know that rank early in my teaching at UBC in the 1960s. At Hamburg University the beginning instructor actually, and rather menially, assisted the professor – by cleaning his blackboard, for instance, or carrying his briefcase. Good for us that this old world university practise had not crossed the Atlantic. The system that gave me unbelievable liberty as a student in Hamburg had its dark side, a strong hierarchy and authoritarianism within the professorate.

Between lectures, in my little room, on the train back and forth to the Dammtor station, I read: Toynbee, Cervantes, Bullock's book on Hitler, Gullwitzer's account of his experiences in Russia, Goethe's Faust, and Thomas Mann's *Tod in Venedig* (Death in Venice). On Jan 27, 1955 the diary says, "His words really 'lie down together'." Fifty-six years later I have Mahler's 5th symphony, *A Death in Venice*, ready to hand in our Honda Odyssey.

The need to read widely, to pick up on literature cited by professors, suggested in reviews, featured in the windows of bookstores, or urged by a friend, reading as a default occupation, this has lasted a lifetime. Into 1954–55, I also crammed in as much good music as possible.

Fifteen curtain calls

Evenings in Hamburg were often spent at concerts: symphonies, a comic opera, even a full scale opera, *The Marriage of Figaro* no less. The Berlin Philharmonic with Karajan was memorable: "Mozart, Strauss and Brahms, hence quite easy for me to understand and enjoy."

I was especially taken with the pianist, Walter Gieseking.

"I had been able to get a ticket at a student rate for an overflow chair on the podium, from where I could see very well the hands, the keyboard and the face of this artist as he played … He never once changed his facial expression of inscrutable austerity all through the concert … He seemed entirely bound up in his music and that any expression had to come via that medium – it did. His body had gone on in years and he was finding it difficult to execute striking voluminous parts without short gasps … His hands fascinated me, they were like mobile pieces of sculpture. Every knuckle moved smoothly. The tips of his fingers always seemed to descend with a gracefully restrained yet determined sweep. They always seemed to just touch the keys … I noticed a precision of tonal modulation, a sensitivity to the aire, the core and theme of his selection. When he broke into a theme it just simply swept one away ... The finale was impressive: fifteen curtain calls. I had never witnessed such adulation of an artist before."

An apparition

A girl I knew at home ghosts through my diary. I was at a concert and I don't remember what was on the program but I do remember clearly that I had a seat angled to a flight of other seats and there was her face, not really, but I saw her. Nothing came of that friendship, but it might have if my friend had ever been able to throw back her head as did the girl before me, shake off her melancholy, look openly and freely at the world.

Movies

In high school, Franz Thiessen read us Erich Kästner's fine German story: *Emil und die Detektive*, i.e. Emil and the Detectives. In Hamburg I got to see the movie. Emil is sent by his mother to take some money to his grandmother, the cash pinned to the lining of his jacket. It was stolen and then retrieved with the help of some street kids, the 'detectives'. When I finally got the money I had waited for in Athens, as I'll explain, I remembered the story and left the city with a wad of one hundred US one dollar bills pinned to the lining of my jacket with a safety pin.

Other serious things

During the winter I worked on a self-assigned essay regarding the nature of the discipline I had chosen. As it developed I recognized the worm that was turning in my apple: discrepancy between scientific evidence regarding the origin of things that I was just becoming aware of and the scriptural account. "Whether or not biblical accounts ... seem to be in harmony with science. God is in harmony with science, of that I am sure." I would soon be much less sure. I never did finish the paper and was embarrassed about this, here was my university time streaming by and I couldn't finish even one paper, but then nobody had set me a topic or deadline; there would be no mark, none of the accustomed pressure. I really was between two university systems, exempt from the exigencies of both – an unsettling but delicious space. It was an opening for dissipation, barred to me by spiritual conditioning. I wish now I had found in the diary some breach in the young man's sanctimony, at least a reference somewhere to having cut loose; it isn't there.

In late November I got grim news from home, my parents had had an auto accident and were severely injured. A discussion followed as to whether I should drop everything and come home to help, but the decision was to stay. The accident gave the rest of 1954–55 an edge.

Warmth and strong support is what I remember most about my home. Mary, my sister, is on the left, then our parents Eva and John. We're on the UBC campus, in front of Brock Hall. I was the first among my kin on both sides to take the risk of going to university, or to put it differently, to take the opportunity. My parents were not able to support my university studies financially, but they approved of my going and helped in many moral and practical ways.

Our home was very Mennonite Brethren, an evangelical wing of Mennonitism that originated in Russia, and pious but not too repressive. A personal religious experience was emphasized and had been affirmed by adult baptism. We acknowledged the religious and social strictures that came with this persuasion, we didn't go to movies and we didn't dance, but we discussed the tenets at home on many occasions and worried our share over church politics. We were made aware of the great travail of Russian Mennonitism in the early twentieth century; I would be hearing and reading about it all my life.

The physical and psychological effects of the accident on my parents would overshadow my correspondence with them from here on. I was fully sympathetic, I thought, but by mid-January I was confiding to my diary that I had to guard what I said in my letters and yet try not to compromise the truth. This plus the high emotional tones and my saccharine religious language has lessened my interest in the packets of correspondence in my files. In them I was making the case for how it was all worth it. Eventually, however, it was necessary for me to go home several months earlier than I had planned.

I was always very fond of my sister Mary, we seldom fought as I remember it now but that may be selective memory. We empathized in our teens and early twenties regarding religious and social issues. She frequently found herself in my shadow, which cannot have been pleasant: I write that with hapless regret. However she always put a good face on this, never lost her graciousness. The accident put a considerable burden on Mary, she had to become prime caregiver. In addition, she was asked to help her brother by moving emergency funds from Canada to Italy and Greece when I was in trouble there.

O Tannenbaum

For Christmas of 1954 I was invited into the home of the Sundermeyers in Bünde, a town southwest of Hamburg. There was a genial program, of which I don't remember the details, to provide a home Christmas for students from abroad. Bells rang on Christmas Eve, the streets were snowy. We did traditional German things, had some glasses of wine, played games. I had a good chat with Ohma, third from the left, trying to enlarge her view of Canada which she thought of as some terribly Nordic place, *"dort oben"*. I'd like to reach into the picture and tap the right shoulder of the young man in the Harris Tweed. Don't crowd out the genial man of the house, Fritz Sundermeyer, head of a firm that makes cigars! Bünde was famous for its cigars.

I had a particular spiritual concern that Christmas. The oldest son, Karl, fourth from the left, who had organized this visit for me, was a committed Christian. Eventually, I understand, he became a missionary.[35] He and I prayed together in a frigid upper bedroom, where I was quartered. I wanted to become an effective Christian, one who would finally 'lead others to Christ'. In no more than ten years, during studies for my Anthropology minor at the University of Wisconsin and after some awkward encounters with protestant missionaries during my early field work in Mexico, I cringed at the recollection of the proselytization that I had once regarded as imperative.

Among old cufflinks, tie-clasps and pins I found my VCF insignia, already up there on the lapel of the Harris Tweed on a previous page. The symbolism is aggressive, out of the book of Ephesians in the New Testament. Red is for the blood of Christ, the only means of salvation, mediated by the cross. The 'sword of the spirit' – for defence, for proselytization! The shield of faith. Seems to me now as benign radicalization, which is and is not a contradiction.

I also found a worn little guide to devotions; the young man had marked a personal objective: "There is a passion for Christ which it has been given to very few to possess, but which has set those who have it apart for ever from their fellow men".[36] He meant to realize that passion, to know God's will; he aspired to discipleship – he'd been reading Bonheoffer on this subject. Various of his contemporaries couldn't follow him in this, some, I know, regarded him as presumptuous and egotistical.

Regret

The young man was too earnest by half. I wish that somewhere, somehow, during his undergraduate years he had learned moderation in belief and conduct, moved a little beyond dichotomous thinking, beyond categorizing people as ins or outs. Some of his friends already knew then about the wisdom of moderation in matters of faith. He didn't appreciate it until later.

Sometimes, during the many years that I travelled in Latin America and taught in various universities, especially when I had members of Roman Catholic orders in my seminars, I would feel envious: Why couldn't I have been born into a less demanding Christianity? It baptized you, let you confess and be absolved, it married you and buried you. *Salud!* This was idle on my part, since I was thereby probably belittling the spirituality of my RC friends and disregarding the strength of my own conditioning. Ritualized religious practice was basically alien to me.

This regretful line of thought was amplified during the development of this memoir by a brief excursion into philosophy, for which I had never had much time. A new book had appeared, James Miller's *Examined Lives: From Socrates to Nietzche*. I was certainly 'examining', so this was probably relevant. For the first time I came on the French philosopher, Montaigne.[37] I pursued him through two biographies and into his famous *Essays*; I found my own regretful recollection of uncompromising Christianity of the young man engagingly pointed up by Montaigne. As Miller has it, "[Montaigne] thought it possible to 'love virtue too much'. The 'fairest souls,' he suggests, are supple, flexible, prepared to negotiate complex and changing circumstances ... Sobriety entails moderation in belief and conduct, the opposite of ... unyielding conviction and resolute consistency." [38]

International student

In the Sundermeyer home that Christmas, and at the University of Hamburg anyway, I was that sort of a student. I became sensitized to what separation from family and culture meant and how important a temporary new community could be. When I got back to UBC I became quite involved with students from other countries, particularly the two Brits who were also doing an M.A. in our Geography Department. From friendly contacts with students of other religions I sustained doubts about the exclusivity of the Christianity that I advocated; these would not go away. Jesus is to have said: "I am the way, the truth and the life; no man cometh unto the Father but by me." (John 14: 6) One can't very well be crediting international friends' cultures and religions and maintain the exclusivity of evangelical Christianity.

International students were most agreeably hosted at the University of Hamburg, helped in all manner of ways, and taken on excursions by the administrators responsible for us. On January 6, 1955 I got to ski for the first time, in St. Andreasberg, an idyll in the Harz Mountains. I do not have my skiing friend's name; I vaguely recall he was from India, but I remember clearly that we had a good time, and of course I was in my very Canadian, back-woodsy mackinaw, topped by the Québécois beret.

The excursion was rich with 'Sehenswürdigkeiten', the regional sights, and with conviviality; it included a ramble through Goslar, the town to which I would bring my family to live in 1967 while I worked on Latin American materials in several excellent libraries in Hamburg and Berlin. I would borrow the books, work on them in Goslar and then bring them back. It was like living in a postcard, learning something of a small German town's ways. I even produced a family letterhead. Out of the work would eventually come what I have been told is a good book.

The Auslandsstudenten, the international students, were taken to the Volkswagen plant at Wolfsburg. I enjoyed watching the cars take shape; the worldwide phenomenon they would become was clearly cranking up. We were given lunch in a fine manner;

part of each setting was a delicate glass of Aquavit, a traditional Scandinavian spirit. I spilt mine right off, but was brought another and quite liked it.

Here I am reminded of acerbic Irmy Klassen, long deceased and wryly remembered, who predicted before I left that in Europe I would learn to appreciate alcohol. No, I wouldn't, but I did, especially the aperitif and the digestif, the strongly flavoured medicinal or celebratory jolt. At some home in Northern Germany to which my Mennonite friends from Hamburg took me, we were offered little glasses of *Doornkaat*, a *schnapps*. I got mine down the wrong throat and thought I would die, but showed no sign. I tried it again later and liked it. When I was hitchhiking in southern Italy, on my way to Greece, a motorist took me to his home and before he went to take care of something, poured me an emerald green liqueur, just right for the moment. I have always had something like that in my house.

Lüneburger Heide

There were many journeys out of Hamburg with my Mennonite friends; it would be tedious to try to disentangle them now, in some memories it's cold, in others it's warm. I was always in good company, gathering thoughts on landscapes and human habitation, usually in a spiritual framework, full of the joy of it all.

It's early in the morning en route to a weekend retreat, we're south of Hamburg. My friends are in high conversation. There's little heat in the low-powered early model VW 'Kombi' van. Outside, at intervals, are the characteristic farmhouses, the 'Bauernhöfe,' of the sort already brought to mind by my climatology professor. There was more. We were into the 1950s and Germany's 'economic miracle' was underway; farms were modernizing. The one on the next page had evidently been expanded and probably improved in its equipment and management but was holding to the trusty Holstein breed, prime milk-producer in the temperate world.

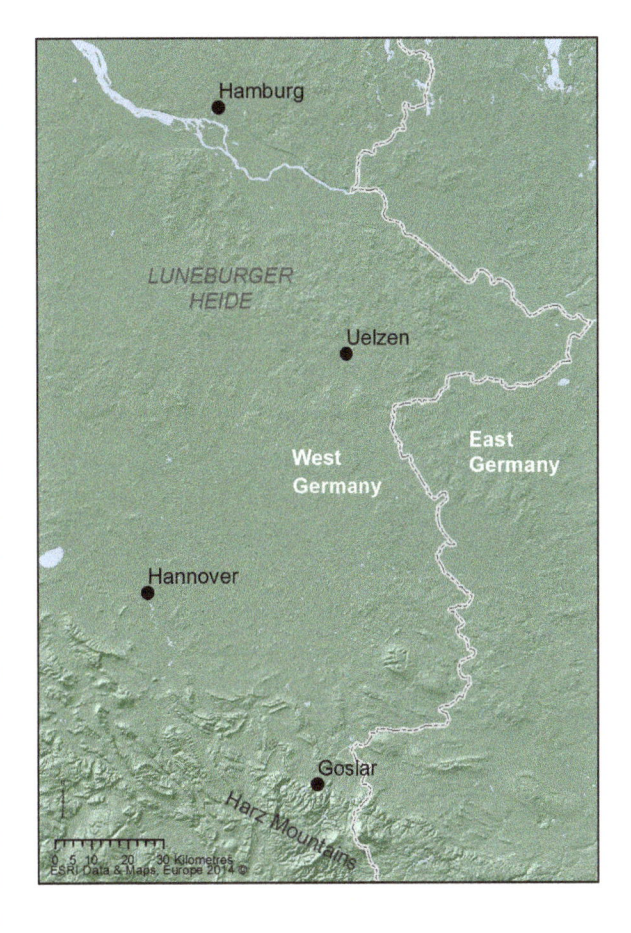

Alfred H. Siemens

Some lines down in the diary I come on a ploughman and his team moving over the brow of a hill, against the sky. "Plodding on and yet not servile" he seemed to me that morning. "Content in that old, old agricultural tradition, the land a kindred thing." I would come on just such a scene in Mexico, years later. In numerous fieldtrips and discussions, especially those in my seminars in the Anthropology Department at the Universidad Iberoamericana in Mexico City we came to think critically of the peasant condition, but didn't lose respect nor an aesthetic affinity for the traditional.

The physical basics of the heathland are only indicated in the diary, I still had limited conceptual resources with which to work, but they can be easily detailed now: gentle undulations and flat land, sandy soils underneath, all attributable to the last glaciers.[39] A low shrub vegetation, dotted with trees and seasonally graced by purple heather alternates with woodland. What I didn't fully appreciate then is that this is an anthropogenic landscape. It was often burned over and cultivated from about 3000 BCE onward until the soils were degraded and carried only shrub vegetation. Heather itself is evidently quite resistant to fire and grazing. The heathland or *Heide* as a whole still supports some grazing, a good part of it has been set aside as a nature reserve and some is laced with tank tracks. When I came by in the mid-1950s testing and training grounds had been laid out for the new German army, they were not yet on the maps I carried. The *Heide* is surrounded and interspersed by cultivation and settlement, which is mostly what one sees as one travels through the region.

Sounds like a geographical fieldtrip narration, it's the way I would have talked if I had had the chance to bring students here.

I found ancient stone structures, which are sometimes called 'Dolmen;' sometimes 'Hünengräber,' meaning the graves of giants.[40] They apparently date back about three millennia before Christ and probably were not really graves but rather cult foci. In any case I was impressed by their dramatic masses and enigmatic simplicity.

This was an early whiff of prehistory, which I would become heavily involved in later. I would become a geographer who consorted with archaeologists, who specialized in the aerial search for pre-Hispanic agricultural remains in wetlands and groups of monumental mounds, as along the coastal margin of the region of Los Tuxtlas in the Mexican state of Veracruz.[41]

Alfred H. Siemens

By the end of the winter semester in Hamburg there were other whiffs. I was thinking south and lemon blossoms. In late February I was on my way.

MONDAY, FEBRUARY 28, 1955

'Kennst du das Land wo die Zitronen blühn?'

A bit antique and sentimental to quote Goethe? No question, but the words are still evocative. It goes on from that first line:

Im dunklen Laub die Goldorangen glühn,
Ein sanfter Wind vom blauen Himmel weht,
… Dahin! Dahin

You can't translate this closely, but it more or less raises the question of whether one wouldn't rather be where the lemon trees bloom, where oranges glow out of dark foliage and soft breezes blow? Germans stuck in their grim winters have habitually longed to go south, and so did I.

In late February of 1955 I prepared; I bought something between a bicycle and a wimpy motorcycle, called a *moped*, and planned to do my Mediterranean tour on it. The weather was snowy and cold in northern West Germany, so I shipped the moped ahead to Munich and followed by train. It was in fact damaged in transit, but a continuation southward across the even snowier Alps on such a contraption looked foolhardy anyway, so I stored it in Munich, to be picked up and fixed on my way back. I intended now to travel south on the train and on my thumb, which I did. The moped served me quite well later on various particularly enjoyable road trips in central West Germany, in spite of torn control lines, flat tires and clogged plugs.

Coming north over the Alps in spring of 1987, after a conference in Rome, I saw a vast panorama of snowed ridges out of my window and recalled how I had planned to cross them on my moped in 1955. I would have killed myself.

Alfred H. Siemens

From an entry in my diary on February 27: "I am on my way again ... alone but not at all dismayed, because actually I am not alone. *He* goes with me." Admirable in the context, I'm sure, but here and now I need to use other words. The adventure can just as well be accounted for by a combination of initiative, certainly, ingenuity enough to compensate for frequent stupidities, curiosity always, the odd bit of good luck, and the kindness of strangers. Most everyone seemed to be well disposed toward a clean-cut young Canadian.

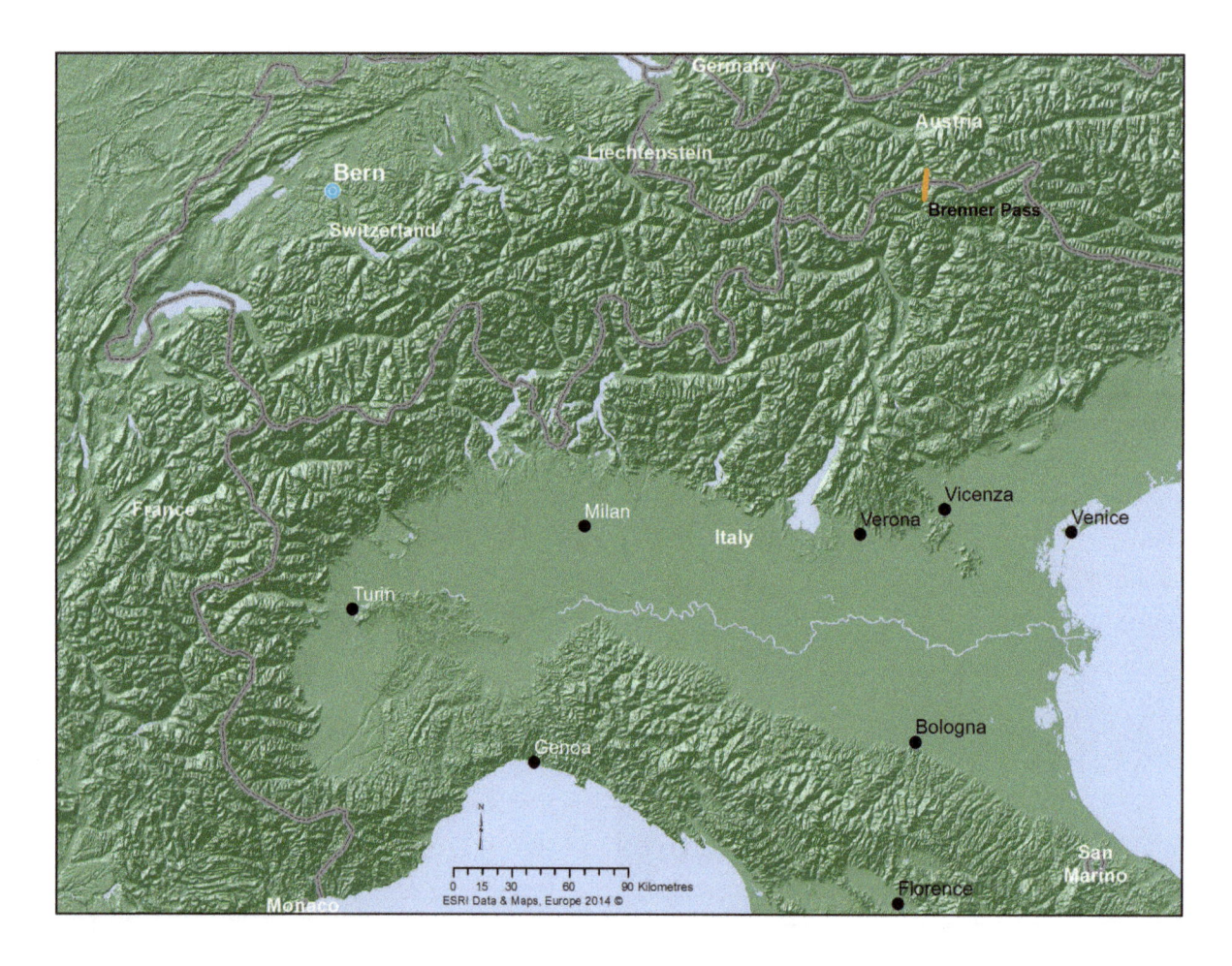

An important boundary lay just ahead, after crossing a bit of Austria I would enter Italy. This had long meant escaping cold northern airs and stultifying customs. The Mediterranean south was somewhat disorderly and disreputable, certainly, but evocative to the versifiers and the painters – a different light, a different life. Later, I would come to appreciate that the meaning of this border for northern Europeans was not unlike the meaning, for North Americans, of going down to Mexico and thus entering Latin America. Various European travellers into the Americas explicitly made the comparison between Italy and Mexico.[42] It was the great North American alternative. Tired of a woman? Killed a man? Can't stand the winter one more day? Want to write a novel? Go south.

Reconstructing this departure I realize it's happening again, the agreeable assembly of the best available materials for a given journey or the writing of the journey later. Maps are fetishes for me, as I've said. Perhaps it's just that I'm directionally challenged. I carry a Boy Scout compass in my vest pocket on flights and in my vehicles at all times, just to check. On research journeys I've carried successive generations of GPS receivers and resorted to satellite images, particularly as made accessible by Google Earth. On guided post-retirement journeys with Alice, I've usually had better materials than our guides. One just puts together the necessary information plus something poetic like a bit of Goethe.[43]

Once over the Brenner Pass I noticed "lilting" Italian coming from the railway station P.A. system. In the landscapes that passed the window, there was grime and "tumble-downness". Housing had changed from steeply gabled alpine to flatter tile-roofed Mediterranean. There were vineyards and swarthy people.

I had a vivid encounter in Vicenza, my first stop in Italy. The diary slides over it but memory has kept it as a curio to be taken down and smiled over, as here now between my keyboard and my monitor. I knew no Italian, but had written down the name of an inexpensive hotel from my guidebook. "I was a bit apprehensive, but then I committed all to the Lord and stopped worrying." I just went up to a policeman at an intersection with my bit of paper. He saluted me and then mimed a question, I bless him still, raising his eyebrows and then inclining his head on his hands, as on a pillow. I nodded vigorously, by which time onlookers had become interested. Stay where you are, he indicated. When the right bus came along he stopped it, had a word with the driver and beckoned me aboard. Result: I was soon well and economically ensconced, convinced again of divine guidance.

Nothing left to say

Already in the fifteenth century someone complained that Venice was a city "about which so much has been said and written ... that it seems to me there is nothing left to say."[44] But there is. A first sight makes the well-known, this city, Stratford-upon-Avon, wherever, necessarily interesting. I need to watch that last word. In my Master's oral exam at UBC in 1958, Lew Robinson faulted me on my overuse of it and I have had to swat it out of my prose ever since. Maybe it's just a verbal tick, but when I look at the word in the OED, it is said to mean: "Having the qualities which rouse curiosity, engage attention or appeal to the emotions." It's good to find such places and maybe the word is not such a bad tick to have.

Alfred H. Siemens

I didn't ride a gondola, I couldn't afford it but scorned it nevertheless as touristic. I hadn't seen the changing of the guard in London either. I wasn't like every other tourist. I would, however, get to see the pope in Rome. Thus one ticked off the 'sights' of Europe, or not.

Venice, and Italy, struck me as grubby. A "pall of inevitable and sure decay hung everywhere." But how perversely attractive, too. It was still chilly in Venice, there were traces of snow in the corners. The green mackinaw would have been just the thing but I had left it in Hamburg expecting warmth.

St. Mark's: "For a very long time I had wanted to enter this church ... however the inside was very disappointing. I had imagined something grand to equal the façade. Instead there was grey disintegration on every hand. Just ahead an old priest was saying mass. Up in the arches somewhere to the right, stone masons were tap-tap-tapping. Upwards of say fifteen feet almost every square inch of surface is covered by one huge mosaic ... scenes of infinite variety ... To the common man this will all at one time have been an educational spectacle ... The floor is extremely uneven, in places visibly wet. Sagging foundations have tilted and cracked pulpits, pillars and posts. All is grey, grimy and overrun by tourism." Later I would read that the undulation of the floor was planned in order to represent stormy water —Venice in peril.[45] I doubt it.

Wandering through the streets one has to take note: such a pedestal, such a horse, such a man, Bartolomeo Colleoni, a meritorious captain-general of Venice in the fifteenth century.

There have been many subsequent trips to Europe and it has always been satisfying and renewing to look again at old European stone, at pillars, pediments, textured surfaces, escutcheons and garlands, carved allusions to the famous and prosperous.

I also happened on a construction site. A palace had been torn down and foundations were being pounded in for a new one, the whole project "shabby, oozy and sticky." It was already common knowledge that the city was sinking, I'm not sure that it was yet appreciated that the sea was rising as well. Here in late 2010 there is news of extraordinary flooding in downtown Venice. You walk on temporary catwalks in tall boots, which can be quite striking under a short skirt.

My scrabble through galleries intensified in Italy. Here in Venice, Renaissance painting got a swipe in the diary: "Flesh, flesh, flesh; it's disgusting, especially the endless succession

Alfred H. Siemens

of voluptuous females, gored bodies of Christ, spiked Sebastians and straw-cradled babes in Bethlehem." I would come on masses of such art again years later in Madrid but I found that by then I had become more appreciative of it.

One rides the vaporetto along the Grand Canal and admires the architecture. This, I found out later, is the Palazzo Cavali- Franchetti. It has been renovated and has lost the seedy charm it had for me in 1955.

Everyone thinks of Thomas Mann in Venice, he wrote the famous melancholy novella *Death in Venice*, which was adapted into various other media. And everyone gets lost. I have strong recollections of labyrinthine wandering and the play of light. Shafts of sunlight found their way through narrow passages, on to shuttered windows and their boxes. Somewhere canaries sang. Mondays were Mondays here too evidently; new washing dangled above. Suddenly a canal would open up, a bridge lifted one for a pleasant look left and right and then plunged one down into the next dark passage. At dusk, warm indirect light enlivened the pastel palaces and soon, in the distance, one could make out the lights of the Lido.

On my rail ticket through Italy I could get off and on again, and trains were frequent. Thus, on the way from Venice toward Rome, I stopped in Bologna. It was streaming miserable Mediterranean winter rain and I suddenly I found that I had had enough of hard scrabble travelling and my diet of found edibles. I marched into a classy restaurant and began to order, everything from appetizer to dessert. So, there in my entry for March 9, 1955, I'm eating "delicious spaghetti with meat sauce". I have had "spaghetti bolognes" hundreds of times since; it is the one Italian dish I really like and I had quite forgotten where I first had it. So I did cut loose, once, moderately.

Diligent again

What I could see out of the window as we went southward from Bologna up into the Apennines toward Rome just was not enough. I needed to get out into the rural landscapes passing by. Hardly any experience of 1954–55 throws such a long shadow into the future. I stood by the door of the rail carriage, pack in hand – it was a local that stopped at every station. I watched till I saw an intriguing scene and then quickly got off when the train halted for a few minutes. I could always get on the next train and continue my journey toward Florence and Rome.

Alfred H. Siemens

I became aware of particular house forms, domesticated plants, a production system, the green of spring in a Mediterranean land and rural sounds. Sitting before these images now, I find myself 'reading' them again, looking for evidence of irrigation, the actual crops, noticing the pollarded tree next to the house, the details of the house form itself, the hay stack, the people that may well be watching me and so on, just as I have done it for decades now with a diligence that I can't assume many others share but that I remain ready to advocate. And up there on the ridges, the country homes of urbanites? In these Apennines views I also became more aware of the landed estate, the *latifundium* of the Latin world. I had little information yet with which to interpret this specific instance or to flesh out the concept but I would gather a great deal more in the years ahead as I travelled in Spain and Latin America.

Green Mackinaw

86

Alfred H. Siemens

Shoe leather for Florence

Florence was next, I trudged in and around it for the best part of five days, saving on streetcar fares to buy food and noting the wear on my footgear each night. You could get into museums for very little if you could show you were a student. The sometime student of art with a work ethic now entered fully into Mediterranean due diligence: museums, churches, painters and sculptors, item after item ticked off. This looks a bit frenetic or pedantic, one or two friends still see my antics that way. In any case Prof. Binning was fully corroborated, it was all here and it was fascinating – aesthetic terms of reference for a lifetime.

Brunelleschi's dome was the engineering wonder of his day and bellwether of the Italian Renaissance. From it one surveys the city, and sure enough, there is the Medici Palace, notable expression of the Renaissance and monument to a dynasty.

On the Piazza della Signoria, not far from the palace, I found the spot where Savonarola was burned at the stake. I had to wipe mud off the name with my shoe so I could get an intelligible image. He was a fiery preacher and an uncompromising Dominican friar, a critic of the Renaissance, of the Medici rulers of Florence and of the pope; he proclaimed the Last Days.[46] Savonarola was famously responsible for what is called the 'Bonfire of the Vanities' – books, immoral paintings, vain clothing, musical instruments, all were gathered up and burned on the same plaza where he would be burned. Eventually he came to govern the city himself, but there were mob protests against him, no doubt machinations of incredible complication, this was Florence after all. Pope Alexander VI ordered his arrest and execution in 1498.

Alfred H. Siemens

At the foot of Brunelleschi's dome I found closely packed old Mediterranean buildings cohering into an immensely pleasing array of forms. This can be called *settlement morphology*. Does that sound ponderous? I mean the wonderfuly variegated structures that people build in towns and in the country as they occupy an area, as they settle in, structures that bear the imprint of culture, that testify to the passage of time, that embody inumerable practical adaptations and successions of technology, that are sometimes crass and graceless, but often imaginative and aesthetically delightful, too. The material edges over into the poetic. It would happen repeatedly during my year abroad and for the rest of my life, as in eastern Morocco in 2010, among well-weathered kasbahs, the stongholds of prominent families.

One can cover a lot of ground in a five-day walkabout, crossing the Ponte Vecchio, for example, the Medieval bridge that spans the Arno, built over by shops selling jewellery, art and tourist kitsch. I walked out to the Pitti Palace and the Boboli Gardens, I went back and forth through the centre of town, past Ghiberti's very fine Gates of Paradise, i.e. the doors of the Baptistery near the cathedral.

And of course, there was much Michelangelo, including the statue that requires no caption. For me his most impressive sculptures were the unfinished slaves in the Gallerie dell'Accademia:[47] "Out of the rough marble these substantial figures were seeking desperately to free themselves. The … muscles in violent strain seemed almost to have succeeded."

Alfred H. Siemens

Uneven arches

From Florence I took a train northwest to Pisa; two things take up most of that day's space in the diary: The first was my enjoyment of the main buildings. The Romanesque style has fascinated and pleased me wherever I have come on it since. Usually it's rhythmic and consistent as here too at first sight but then delightfully uneven on closer examination. There's the big leaner, of course, as well as the corners that are off plumb, the arches unevenly arched and spaced and the nave that seems to depart from the level.

The more important issue in the Pisa entry was a reflection on photography of the uninformed, superficial sort. "I am determined to prevent ... a mania for pictures. I realized today just what it could do. It prevents delightful 'Besichtigung' [deliberate observation] and arouses a need to capture, to possess immediately. To photograph and later display any feature of the landscape one has not properly understood or appreciated is really hypocrisy."

The entry in the diary goes on to describe the obviously thoughtless tourism and photography that went on around me that day. I would be sensing this disgust all my life, sometimes it would spoil important places for me and I would have to leave, or I might turn to photographing the antics of the people around me. This could become satire or a valuable bit of ethnography. In some recent travels with

Alfred H. Siemens

Alice I experimented with a hands-in-the-pockets, carefree whistling kind of tourism: just looking, no shooting. It worked fairly well during walks in Wales, in the Ukraine and Russia, and in South Africa. However, I have to admit that Alice always carried a point-and-shoot camera in her purse – a gift from me, and I sometimes borrowed it! After a few years I found I was missing too many visual opportunities and soon shouldered again the black knapsack with the photographic impedimenta.

Shadows high on the walls and men muttering in their dreams

Slides of Rome, I had a fair series of them when I came home and they got me good responses. As I've worked with their digitized versions here, enhanced their colour and contrast, trimmed them and touched them up, I can recall the satisfaction of first coming on the coliseum, the Castel Sant'Angelo near the Tiber, and St. Peter's, of course, which I couldn't just photograph straightforwardly, now could I?

However, in my diary and recollections the bright colourful Rome of the slides is more like the black and white city of Vittorio De Sica's film, *The Bicycle Thief*. My stay was overshadowed by a preoccupation: I was running out of money, my scholarship payment had not reached me as planned. I stayed in a very modest Roman Catholic hostel for impecunious men – even cheaper than the regular youth hostels – hidden among the dark, grubby but piquant streets of a poorer part of the city not far from St. Peter's. The hostel was a warren of fibreboard cubicles, open at the top, within one large room that was originally an annex to a church. Figures of various popes, indifferently sculpted, looked down from every side. Our lights were the smallest electric bulbs I had ever seen, just a few inches long, but they were enough to angle shadows from the churchmen on to the walls and the ceiling, I could write in my diary and read.

Alfred H. Siemens

From there I sallied, undeterred, on foot for ten consecutive days, to such a list of museums and churches that just to read of it all now is tiring. I even trudged out some distance along the old Roman Road, the Appian Way, which leads on to the heel of the boot, which was where I would be going soon.

I had two good guidebooks, which have gone missing in shakedowns of my library. I also carried a miniature King James Bible given me by my parents, which I still have. It fit well into the top right pocket of the Green Mackinaw and can just be detected in the photograph of the novice on the back cover of this book. It feels good in the hand even now; it has dated underlinings, poignant evidence of daily strengthening, notes of joy, graspings of wisdom.

As I wrote or read into each night at the hostel a chorus of snores ascended. Occasionally someone muttered uneasily in their sleep. Motorcycles and little Fiats roared by outside, and there was one now, the diary says. One evening street children yelled outside, next day we saw they'd built a bonfire against our entrance. During the day shabby types shuffled around. People stared at the outlandish foreigner.

By this time in my travels I was regularly feeding myself out of my knapsack: bread, jam, maybe a bottle of juice or milk, no wine yet, fruit, cheese, potato chips, and I was liking it, this ambulatory picnicking – it would become a lasting predilection. Occasionally I had an olive-oily meal of mainly spaghetti, in an inexpensive restaurant. One day someone just outside of the hostel sold me a piece of orange Velveeta cheese out of a wooden box marked: 'A Gift of the American People, Not for Sale'.

Poste Restante

From my first day in Rome to my last day in Athens the most important item on my agenda was always a trek to the main post office and in particular to the department where they kept the mail for those without a permanent address. Soon I had to add regular checks at the American Express office and one or two banks. It became clear to me that my trust in what the charming people at the foreign student administration of the University of Hamburg had assured me that mail and money in the Mediterranean would work as well as they did in Germany, all that had been naive. Mail-outs of money from my scholarship and my home account, or even the telegraphing of funds in case of emergency, were not predictable.

Unfortunately, I had not been in a position to buy travellers cheques ahead of time and did not carry that old traveller's standby, a letter of credit. Anyway, these were for moneyed travellers, not students. There were not yet any bank or credit cards, of course, and thus no ATM's. Repeatedly I had only enough on hand for a few days of bare essentials – heroism by default. But I learned. I would literally never leave home again without adequate means of payment in pocket, preferably several kinds and always including cash. "The effort required for sightseeing when one has such a load on one's mind is ghastly." Here I was in *the* historic city of the world …

and found it difficult to even care about what I was seeing. "But work I must even now, for as work I have come to regard this difficult touring and viewing, and so I set one foot before another. Arriving at a bridge over the Tiber I just stopped and stared into its muddy water, my mind blank." A low point, but of course I soon summoned up enough persistence to go on to St. Peters: the huge piazza before it, Bernini's columns, a vast, high interior, dramatic light, endless marble floors, "beauty and splendour".

Many hapless young people abroad have had to do an intimidating trudge to the nearest consulate. My first dealings with that office were indeed quite frustrating. Enter Edith: I can't summon up her face now, nor remember much about her, but I had met her on my first evening in Rome and she had assured me she would help me if the consulate wouldn't, so I had to ask her and she helped, with a traveller's cheque for ten dollars US, signed. This was wonderful and would help for a while, by which time surely, something would have arrived. However, the banks wouldn't cash an already signed cheque. I happened on Edith that same day in a museum and she was kind enough to come with me to the bank and sign another cheque there in the presence of … etc. It seems now like doggedness and happenstance; then it was all the beneficent leading of the Lord. Before the end of my stay I was able to talk the Canadian consul out of 4000 lire – in the form of a cheque. It turned out to be very difficult to get the consul's cheque cashed as well. Kindness of strangers, sort of.

Various great works of art, a fine range now that I think of it, entered my personal repertoire in Rome; I would resort to them for the rest of my life. The *Belvedere Torso* is one of them.[48] It's a Greek figure dating perhaps to the second century BCE, to be found in the Pinacoteca of the Vatican. "Never such a back."

As it happened I returned to Rome in 1987; I dearly wanted to see this back again, and the Sistine Chapel too. The crush and confusion of visitors in the museums of the Vatican had become such that I never got to see the Torso. I did get into the Sistine Chapel, newly brightened by Japanese restorers. We were let in by batches and made to sit while a voice repeated at short intervals: 'Quiet please,' *'Ruhe bitte,' 'silencio por favor'* and I don't know how many other versions of the same admonition. What remains then of the thrill at seeing God's finger reach out to Adam, the swirl of robes and figures, last judgements and all? Not much.

I'm off on a tangent and I might as well continue. Recollections interfade. The Rome of 1987 is dominated not by money troubles or a pursuit of images but by a dream, bordering on a nightmare, and by an embarrassment.

I had been invited to give a paper on Pre-Hispanic water and land management at an International Symposium on Water for the Future in Rome. The paper was fairly well received and got published,[49] but more important from my present vantage point is a recurring dream of the time: I would become progressively more and more lost in a large city. I could recognize the city from dream to dream but it had no name. One day in my Rome of 1987 I became lost; the dream sequence had become a reality. During my erring about on foot and by bus I suddenly came on an immigrant couple from some Middle Eastern country lost on the street with their child and a huge suitcase; they haltingly asked me for directions! In the ensuing exchange I was somehow able to find myself in the city and help them. My nightmare had been dissolved into theirs and into a happy ending.

And then there was an even more bizarre experience. A friend from high school days, married to an official at FAO in Rome, lent me her car for an excursion southward. I wanted to visit the Pontine Marshes, what with my interest in wetlands.

The trip went well; along the way I saw a line of the 'Pines of Rome' – a nod to Respighi – and stopped to draw them. I got back safely too but it was after dark as I threaded into crooked, crowded central Rome where I was staying, and parked the car in what seemed a safe place. Before going to bed I decided to check on the car; I walked around the parking spot three times. It was not there. Then I spotted the little sign away up somewhere identifying this as a tow away zone. It took a good deal of effort and money to get the car back the next day.

Back in the Rome of 1955 the Mennonite young man with the protestant work ethic was getting down to observing Roman Catholics. I had already learned to duck into an RC church in order to get away from the noise all around me; I even found that crucifixes helped me meditate and pray. But I was disgusted with the slovenliness of the mass and the negligent and mechanical prayer of those around me, for me prayer was "a complete involvement of self in intelligent conversation".

In a chapel opposite the Basilica of Saint John Lateran I came on the Scala Sancta:

Here are to have been preserved a flight of stairs out of the house of Pilate, ascended by the Lord just prior to his death, shedding his blood on them as he went. Up these steps one must proceed on one's knees, but the reward is great, every step means nine years of purgatory less, if that is, one has been in the correct frame of mind. And that's not all. It is possible to obtain similar benefits for the deceased by climbing on one's knees up the flights of stairs to either side of the holy stairs.

I am chagrined now to read, a little further down, "There was sympathy in my heart for these benighted souls. It doesn't do them a bit of good." The earnest, self-righteous VCF-er was making the expected judgement.

In the church of San Pietro in Vincoli I found Michelangelo's statue of Moses. But it was blocked by American tourists, "photographing madly in this dark church-absolutely crazy". Flash was not allowed, of course. I could imagine the murky pictures that would result. It was apparent from their remarks that these people were, "largely clueless [as] to the meaning and insensitive to the effect of the sculpture … When the culture vultures had gone a few of us began to view the thing carefully, from various angles, to perceive some of its meaning and significance. The figure is that of an elderly man, still very hale and hearty, with a mature and disapproving opinion of what went on around him … His ineloquent mouth frowns upon the children of Israel's inconsistency and negative tendencies. His eyes hold a vast store of authority and power … Anatomically, of course, Moses almost lives. "

The third and last church of that day, the 18th of March, was the *Chiesa del Santissimo Nome di Gesú*, the Church of the Most Holy Name of Jesus, the mother church of the Society of Jesus.[50] When I called it up on my monitor here fifty-six years later almost to the day, I was stunned. I had seen such facades all over Latin America. Evidently it epitomizes the High Renaissance and is the precursor of the Baroque, a style meant to awe. Looking up at its ceiling in 1955 I saw, "Exactly the effect the counter-reforming Jesuits wanted to implant in the minds of its subjects ... gold, dark marble to contrast, broken pediments, colourful flowery painting, illusory and spilling out of the architectural elements, figures of angels in every possible and impossible position... violent sculpture groups, vanquishing the reformers, etc. etc."

Not enough churches yet. On the following day I was out to the *Basilica Papale di San Poalo fueri de Mura*, memorable for its lovely Italian name, if nothing else, the Papal Basilica of St. Paul Outside the Walls. It provided me with a delightful surprise. A group of nuns in black came to kneel before an altar. They became a speaking choir, the sort of choir that Mr. Thiessen, the teacher of respectful memory at the Mennonite Educational Institute, where I took my high school, tried to make of a bunch of us. "Their speaking voices blended in a strange, wistfully beautiful harmony that echoed and re-echoed throughout the church. I just stood there fixed. Their prayer ended, they gracefully crossed themselves and moved away ... fluid motions, noiseless, robes flowing ... almost a ballet ... [but]barely off their knees they were smiling to each other and chatting in low tones."

After the nuns, I still had one further 'sight' on my list for that day, the Baths of Caracalla, Roman baths, that is. The image that I found in the collection is pleasing, in the diary I grumbled over the photographic process. "It can be a peace and leisure destroying mania. I was frustrated till I had the right light ... not till then could I go in peace." I would wait for the right light countless times in the years ahead, struggle with the paraphernalia, which often seemed impedimenta, work hard to compose and capture the critical moment. But this happens to be my art. *'No hay remedio'*, my Mexican friends would say, there is no remedy.

I hoped that the 23rd of March would be my last full day in Rome, I had been there ten days and I was ready to go on in the direction of Brindisi, where, in another *Poste Restante* there, I hoped I would finally get my scholarship payment and from where I intended to take a boat to Greece.

Meanwhile, a Low German saying had come to mind. The gist of it is that to have been in Rome and not seen the pope epitomizes a missed opportunity. I couldn't let it happen. There was word that the Holy Father would appear at 12:30 so at 12:20 we were out on the magnificent Piazza, waiting. Preparations for the western Christian Easter were underway, I'd catch the later eastern Christian Easter shortly in Greece. Choir and instrumental music was being used to test the sound system for a High Mass. At 12:30 the double windows up in the top floor of the papal palace did open, some people knelt – not me, I was a protestant - and he, i.e. Pius XII, blessed us all.

On the evening of that last full day in Rome I had just enough money for a few more hostel nights and breakfasts. Earlier I had wandered through ruins around the Palatine Hill, loving it all, the slanting sunshine, subtle shades, the evening song of birds and the peel of bells. In cool archways over old streets I imagined past pageantry. I recalled solos sung in church and sang out the words of those hymns "loudly and confidently" into the evening air among the ruins.

Writing about this in my little cubicle in the hostel, the heads of popes above me, I heard agitated English being spoken at the door, there were some people in difficulty. "I was able to direct them in this way and that, give them a few hints and pack them off on the right street car to the [regular youth] hostel … happy to be able to do something for someone … after others have done so much for me. And now I go to bed, as if everything were in perfect order!"

Alfred H. Siemens

On a train, still far from Brindisi where I expected my hassle to be ameliorated, I was able to open a window and sing, again, "full-voiced into the morning air". The Italian world and all its people seemed bright and attractive though I knew that, even if there were some dollars for me in the port, other money troubles probably lay ahead.

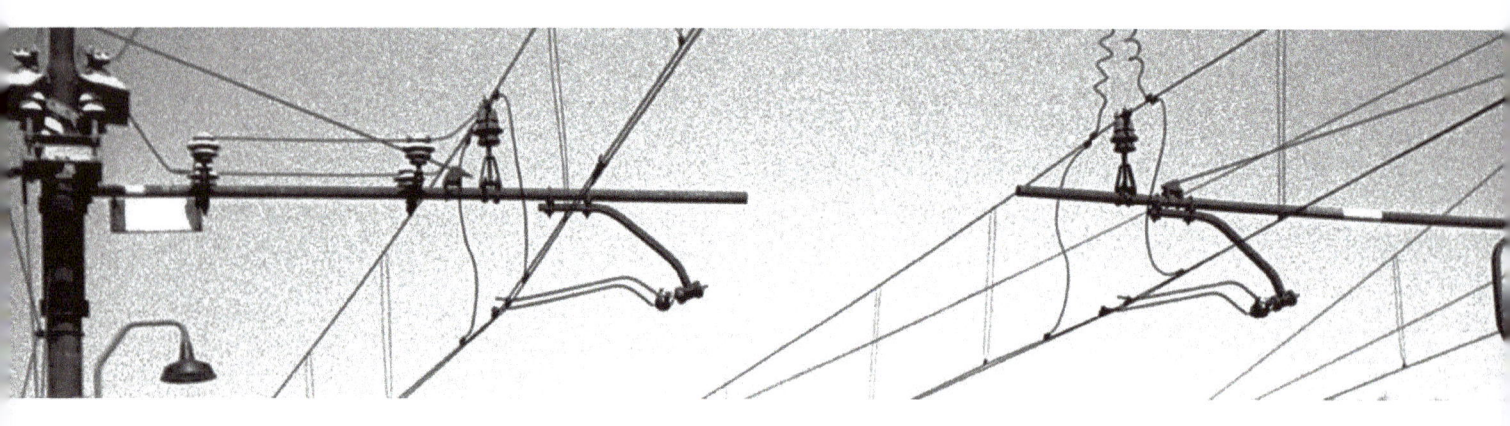

'Music Hour'

The route was now from Rome to Athens via Naples and Brindisi, down into the heel of the boot. In grade school Canadian kids had been made aware of Naples; we learned 'Santa Lucia', a romantic Italian folk song. It came out of a green book called *Music Hour*, with a painting of the lovely arc of the Bay of Naples and Vesuvius in the background, something like what's above.[51] I can hear the melody clearly in my head now and know I sang it often doing farm chores.

Santa Lucia is a section of the waterfront of Naples. Descriptions give the city a thousand marvels, but its reputation for corruption is mentioned too, and we all remember TV footage a few years ago of mountains of Neapolitan garbage that could not be cleared up because of snarled politics. I soon found out that the Santa Lucia of the melodic school song was a rough area but I was determined to walk it, which I did the evening of my arrival with three strong friends acquired in the youth hostel. The account in my diary stutters with disgust, just lists of words and phrases; there's nothing like it anywhere else in the diary. Filth, rubbish, clothes hanging from lines above, ruffians, cocky children swarming the obvious outsiders, selling jewellery, and every kind of souvenir, but also guns and women. Pimps everywhere, kids offering their sisters, whores arguing with Johns. The next day's visit to Pompeii and its evening write-up was a dutiful plod in comparison.

Alfred H. Siemens

Money in Brindizi

Arriving, I went right off to the Poste Restante window in the Post Office. Finally a letter from home; my parents' health and state of mind was improving; Mary was buoyant. Good. And they had cabled me money in Brindisi two weeks ago as I had asked, but where was it? There was no indication in the letter, no notice in the mail. I now became very determined to find it, badgered the various departments of the Post Office itself, searched out exchange and travel bureaus, then banks. What an idea! The foreigner thinks he will find his money has been sent to a bank! A clerk in the Banco Commerzialle finally did agree to ask an accountant who looked at my passport, paused and then said "Si, Si." In a few minutes I had my money. If I had not been dogged I would never have found it.

To Brindisi by train, from Brindisi to Piraeus, the harbour town for Athens, by steamer on a pre-purchased ticket, that was the plan. It left several 'free' days, which I filled most enjoyably hitch-hiking back and forth through Puglia, observing, taking pictures and scribbling in my diary. Freeing up several days in a new place for exploration, as an adjunct to another objective, became a key strategy for the enrichment of my personal geographical repertoire. I had already developed a taste for it before coming to Europe, I would continue it deliberately all my life, wherever I went in the world.

Here in Puglia I was seeing citrus orchards, vines, fig and peach trees, shallow ploughing around the trees presumably for cover crops, cereals and vegetables, many very old olive trees[52] – altogether a venerable landscape.

Stone fences lined the fields: limits but also repositories for stones removed from the fields. Sometimes the fences were of Nopal cactus, a plant that I would see later in Mexico. What a history, plants carried here and there, between the old and the new world, or the reverse, or whatever! Labourers wielded big-bladed, heart-shaped and short-handled hoes. How was it that these back-breaking handles had never been lengthened?

Well heads could be seen at intervals, with wheels to lift the water and animal trudge paths around them. Donkeys carried and pulled. Everything seemed closely settled and worked. The houses were block-like, generally white with green shutters; they mostly had stairs to the flat roofs, which are living spaces. Viewed from a little height and distance they were, "cubes of sugar on dark green satin."

A couple stopped to pick me up; they were going to Alberobello up in the hills, a town with distinctive housing and did I want to come along? This was a gift: "trulli" dwellings, cone shapes very skilfully built of layered stone without mortar.[53] Roofs are a multiple or continuous arch; the outer layer of stones slopes slightly, shedding the rain – an elemental solution to the need for shelter, probably of great antiquity. Each cone surmounts one room; it's topped with a pinnacle and may have one or another of a variety of symbols painted on it. The thick stone walls insulate the interior in cold and hot weather; they last many years. In the decades since I saw them in Puglia northern Europeans have bought and restored many of them. The couple were very good company and made me envious over the way they got along together. I very much wanted a relationship like that.

Roads were filled with FIATs, (evidently there was then a fifty per cent tariff on foreign cars and a governmental subsidy to the national FIAT industry), plus scooters and motorcycles, honking with or without excuses, and the odd large-wheeled cart.

I was travelling just for the pleasure of moving and seeing! The sun was bright, the sky and water were beautiful, it was spring, the most comfortable time in Mediterranean lands, gardens and fields were intensely green. But I was also meeting agreeable people in rapid succession. "Italy is not just landscapes and museums."

Around me in one little place where I had been dropped off well-dressed people were sauntering by, greeting me. I considered myself, my hair uncut, my pants stained. I had become a tramp, but it didn't seem to matter. In a pleasant exchange with a young man, I'll call him Guiseppe, I realized why people were sauntering: it was Sunday, and that hadn't crossed my mind all morning. Of course this triggered a spiritual reflection in the diary, my religion was not dependent on ritual observances.

How could we talk, Guiseppe and I? Language was "reduced to its barest essentials: nouns, verbs, personal pronouns, *and* gestures." Thus we ranged over "Canada, Italy, war, politics, architecture, Italian girls, and war service." Before we parted, he warned me to watch for pickpockets. At another stop I was approached by four very friendly young men. The discussion became quite animated: Where did I come from, how and why? What was it like in Canada? I decided to forget about trying to get a ride and to take a train if I had to. A group was gathering around, some with a good bit of English. Younger boys were edging in keeping eyes and mouths open. The group finally left with a round of handshakes, but two came back in a short while with an English grammar, and we discussed that. Then one of them, who had been the most involved in our discussions, laid out the bottom line: Could I help him to emigrate?

The most striking Puglian encounter is just indicated in the diary with a few mealy words; the nuanced experience rises clearly on reflection. I'm hitch-hiking, a very friendly older man came up to me on his motorcycle and offered to take me to a better stop. OK, he may have had an ulterior motive, but I didn't really care or rather it seems to me now that I was not yet sensitized to homosexual hazards. We sat down on a nearby wall and began to 'converse'. He quizzed me thoroughly about what I was doing and I answered, again in a very reduced language, *with* gestures. We were, after all, in Italy. Then he decided I needed more Italian, found a stick and scratched out words in the dirt before us. I can see, clearly, the smiles with which he accompanied his lesson.

The kindness of strangers. A friendly policeman had helped me to a hostel in Vicenza. I had various congenial rides here in Puglia. A sauve guy in a new Fiat four-door number, a very sensible conversationalist, stopped at his home and poured me an encouragement, a little glass of green liqueur. Then we went on. I rode in the back of an impossibly small Fiat coupe and finally with a very considerate gentleman who took me right up to the pier in Brindisi where the brightly lit *George Potamianos* was tied up. We would be leaving during the night and were free to board.

Before going to sleep I was "given (I'll just quote all this as straightforwardly as I can) a comfort precious and satisfying: 'Be careful for nothing; but in everything by prayer and supplication with thanksgiving let your requests be made known to God.

Alfred H. Siemens

And the peace of God, which passeth all understanding, shall keep your hearts and minds through Christ Jesus.' (Philippians 4:6 and 7)"

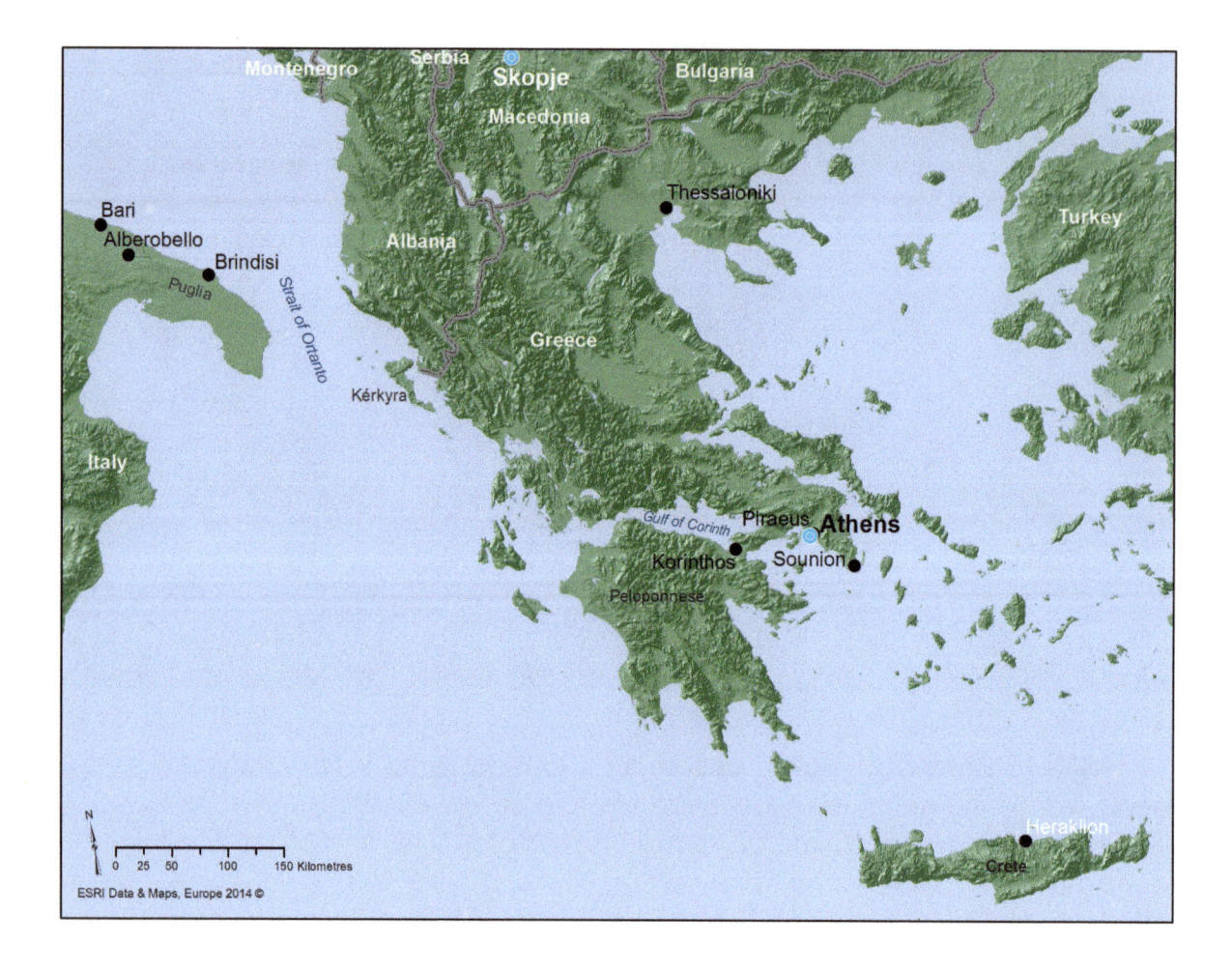

How was this 'gift' brought to mind? Not strange, for someone steeped in the Bible. Embarrassing hocus pocus from my present perspective? Rather, but undeniably reassuring at the time, and with an edifying sound, still. There's a curious immediate sequel in the diary: I was going third class, we had bunks and I happened to be in close quarters with a man who showed suspicious interest in my declaration of money, which one had to fill out in preparation for entering Greece, but "There was really no need to be concerned."

Our ship was to take us across the Adriatic at the Strait of Otranto, stop briefly at the Greek island of Corfu (Kérkyra), then swing around eastward through the Gulf of Corinth and the Corinth Canal, opposite Korinthos on the map, into Piraeus, the port for Athens. I was travelling third class, which entitled me to the bunk in a cabin of four, but also good food and an amiable assemblage of fellow travellers, an "island of English in a sea of Greek". We were up just high enough so that we could look down onto the deck. At Corfu a crowd of Greek passengers came aboard and took possession of that deck with loud voices, strong gestures and vehement expressions.

Years later, when I was analysing the travel accounts of Europeans coming to Mexico in the nineteenth century, I noted how eager many were to read the nature of Mexicans generally from the faces and bearing of the first people they saw when stepping ashore at Veracruz. Here on the steamer and later when going ashore at Piraeus, I was seeing my first Greeks, the most exotic people I had seen so far, and I was looking at them intently. In a few years, during my anthropological studies at Wisconsin I would get to do a lot of reading, contend with my professors over the judgement of other cultures, learn more sensitive designations and gradually assume the tenets of cultural relativism.

Dark country folk had come aboard, some women in peasant dress, most men in 'Western' clothes. They were disposed in every conceivable attitude over all available surfaces. They had brought their own food so there was soon detritus everywhere. I noted chickens and a turkey, and a pungent smell.

Poignant tableaux arranged themselves against the angled deck's architecture. I could imagine how the colours and animated faces might appear in my viewfinder, and my fingers curled, but I just couldn't photograph people straight on. Following them when distracted, as in Victoria station, was one thing, but this seemed too much of an intrusion. I would engrave the images on my mind and honour them with descriptions, I said to myself. This happened to me repeatedly in the years ahead: a line of young Amish boys against a barn in Lancaster County, Pennsylvania, Indians at prayer in the Andes, Tuaregs up from the south in a market in Morocco. Houses and landscapes are comfortably passive by comparison, they don't resent you stealing their souls or grabbing 'shots' that can be sold.

Alfred H. Siemens

Cut slopes

It was good to find this image of the Grecian shore between Corfu and the Corinth Canal, and the corresponding entry in the diary. I was developing an appreciation for environmental history. That term was not in use then, it is the label under which I am rounding off my geographical career now. Aridity was obvious; most striking was the erosion of the shore, the 'hanging' valleys left by the truncation of streams, the whole affected by the long process of weathering, or 'Witterung'. I did not yet remark on the slight remains of a forest cover, the indication of severe deforestation, nor on the probable change of sea level vis-à-vis the land, which was basic to the erosion of the shore. I would later see such processes as 'reduction' of landscapes in many long and densely occupied parts of the world, the backdrops of fighting in Iraq and Afghanistan, for example: worn down by relentless exploitation of resources and natural weathering.

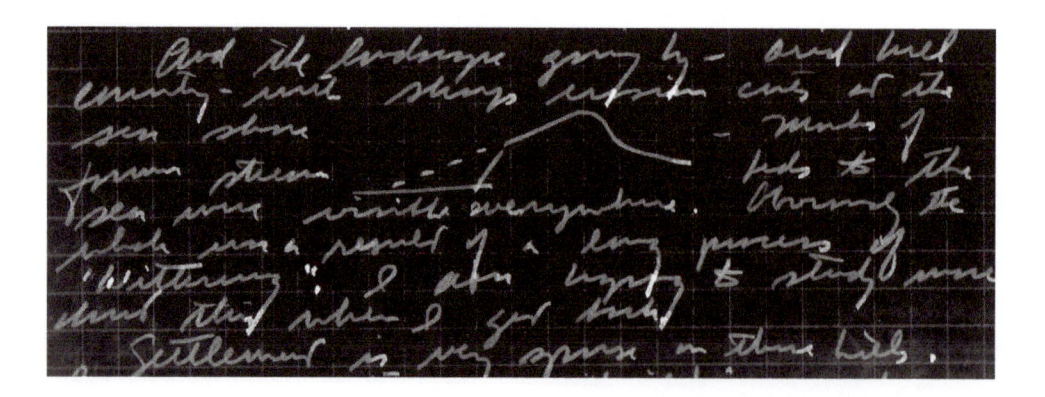

On board in the evening we heard music coming from below and sidled down the staircase between third and deck class: songs with a mood somewhere between wistfulness and melancholy, something strange in the harmony, and dancing too in a pool of light.

Roosters crowed resolutely at dawn of the second day on the *Potamianos* as we were passing slowly through the Corinth Canal.[54] I hear them now as I look at the walls and the water.

TUESDAY, MARCH 29, 1955, GREECE

Sauntering

Coming ashore in Piraeus, Athens' harbour town, we were assaulted as we came down the ramp by men and boys who all wanted to carry our bags, and here's me with a military surplus backpack that I was not about to surrender to anybody. One boy was after me particularly: pinched face, grimy hand stretched out of a sleeve too short, bare feet. Others touted hotels or wanted to get us into one taxi or another, pulling at our clothes, shouts all around. What several other strangers and I needed was to find the train into Athens. We did get there, inquiring for rooms at a hotel in the city we created a sensation again: tourists carrying their own baggage! A policeman had to intervene. In my diary I reflected on the rough tactics one had to assume in order to emerge intact from such situations – quite disagreeable. I was not very sensitized yet to questions of urban poverty and the plight of homeless street children.

I already knew that I would probably face another money problem in Athens. I would have to wait for further remittances from Hamburg and Vancouver, and in the meantime? The city and the surrounding places I was able to get to during my stay of two and a half weeks take shape for me here in my study against moving back images of interfading new friends. Already on the first day there was a guy from Penticton with whom I would wander around the city for a few days; his name has escaped me. Several very fine people lent me money, Stamos, the landowner on the Peloponnesian Peninsula provided a congenial base for several days, followed by Oliver, yes indeed, a spiritual soul mate, and then finally Fred Schwartzman. I had seen him in Florence and he recognized me in Piraeus. In the quick pragmatic banter that ensued he suggested I come to the place where he was staying, the University Club, fifteen drachma a night, a very good price. The lodging, and the new friendship, turned out well. Before long I had had a good meal too, with some sweet 'Samos' wine, which the diary doesn't mention, but which I remember clearly. In my entry for that night I noted that: "Prospects are good. How fortunate to have a heavenly Father!" Indeed.

Some years after I had returned from Europe, but before we were married, I got a card from Alice, which I stapled to a wall. She was telling me to ease up, something she has said to me often since. Some current friends aren't convinced I can do it at all. Well I can and I did during my first days in Athens.

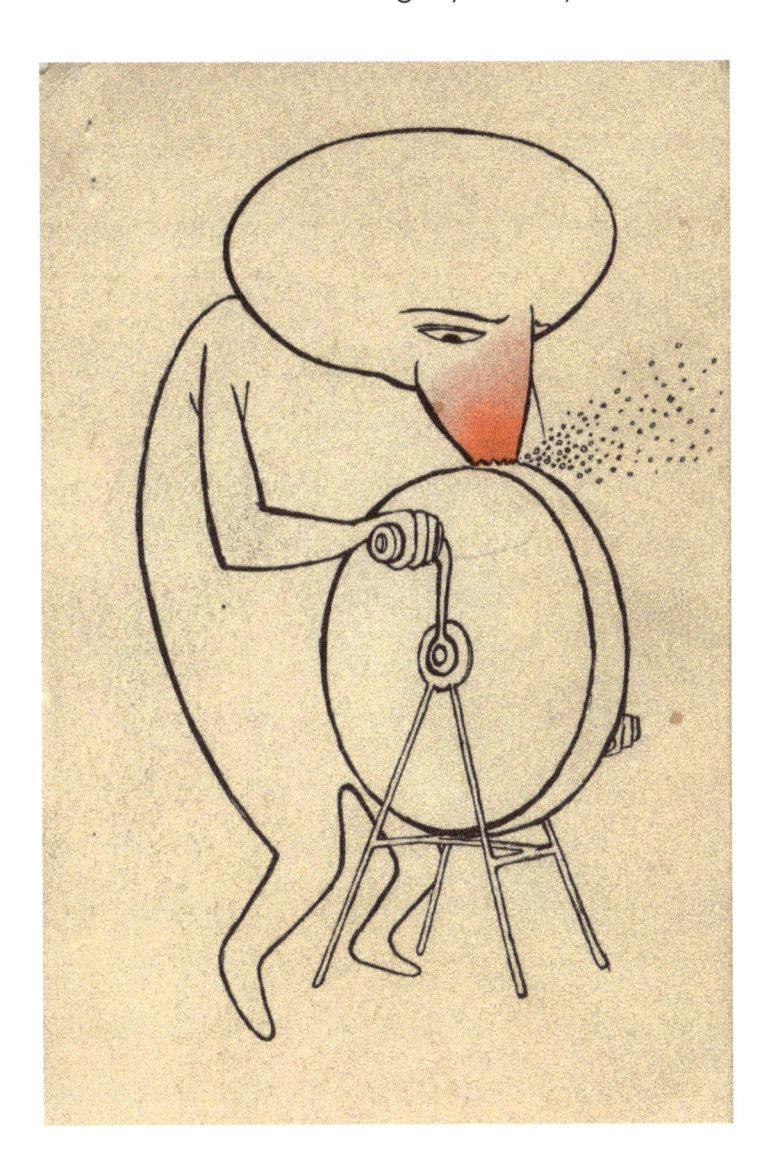

Something had to be done about my pants, I had been able to lay my hands on some cleaning fluid and an iron, I don't remember how. I alternated between two dark shirts of sharp cloth during the whole of the Mediterranean trip and was amazed at how they seemed to remain presentable!

There were lots of other young travellers at the University Club for companionship and information. A good cheap restaurant, the "Ideal" was nearby. After subsisting in Italy on knapsack edibles more or less, I could eat well in Athens: for less than a dollar, for example, I got spaghetti, omelette with sausage, fresh lettuce salad and ice cream. I learned about baklava, I found dried figs and halvah, and came to appreciate sweet Samos wine, as I've said. I tried anise-flavoured Ouzo and the foul turpentine-flavoured Retzina. So, although I had this vague urge to hurry on back to Hamburg and my studies, the money sent me at Brindisi was only a stopgap and I needed to wait for more. Athens wasn't a bad place to wait, as long as there were newly found friends. Had I become a scrounger? Maybe just temporarily, and I did pay my various loans back.

The first thing to do on an orientational saunter has always been to climb up something, a dome, a spire, a hill – like the Lykabettos, in the midst of Athens. It's a steep-sided limestone hill, as is also the hill on which the Acropolis stands. Looking down on a large city you get sounds, maybe an updraft, you sense a pulse, and sniff for a characteristic smell. There was no smog on the morning of my ascent; Athens has since become notorious for it.

Down in the streets there were flowers climbing a wall, an iron fence and balconies that I was given to understand were intimations of the Near East. There was something to this, I found many years later, as I looked along old streets in Istanbul.

The scent of lemon blossoms was actually here; it floated over whole squares. Meanwhile, very persistent shoeshine boys had to be disappointed. I was counting my drachmas carefully; my Grecian adventure was edged by penury. Saying 'no' was complicated by typical Greek gestures. What looked like a nod evidently meant 'no,' when they said 'nai' or did their strange ambiguous diagonal movement of the head, they meant 'yes'.

Who are these three young men at a table under a tree? I have no idea, but I take them now as certainly amused and not unfriendly observers of the foreigners, sauntering.

Alfred H. Siemens

Workshops and stores were clumped by trades, "smithies where iron was being shaped, forges roaring, acetylene torches flickering and hammers pounding." There was a foundry that produced bells and a sequence of coppersmiths, another of shoemakers, "From behind heaps of leather they grinned at us and shouted something." There was a good deal of used clothing and army surplus for sale; one wondered, from whose army and what campaigns?

Doric, Ionic and Corinthian

During the saunter my Penticton friend and I gravitated inevitably to the Acropolis and began to admire the temples. My books had prepared me for the three orders of column capitals that indicated an historical sequence in ancient Greek architecture, the first a flared bowl, the second an open scroll and the third a bouquet of outward curving leaves.

My response to the temples was not a particularly awed approach to antiquity; my German guidebook to Greece had some of that reverence, as I recall. It was lost in one of my downsizings and so I can't check. I was conscious, of course, that here were some of the roots of western culture, and also that in Greece I was approaching both Eastern Europe and the Near East. Mainly I was responding aesthetically, tracing the powerful lines of this famous architecture, appreciating harmonies and perspectives, wandering, clambering over and into, breathing clear blue Mediterranean air, sitting in the shade of some wall, looking out over the city on the one side and then out to sea on the other.

This was impressionistic viewing versus deliberate searching out, identifying and annotation; maybe later. As it turned out I didn't get to it but I did retain a rich set of impressions of essentials. This was a lesson: the details were always there in reference books, now they're on the web. A strong mind picture, and perhaps a photograph or three, perhaps a sketch, were what you wanted to take away, not a detailed report.

We went up into the Acropolis[55] through the main gate, the Propylaea, and found it was a slow day for photographers in front of the Erechtheion. We were no good to them, we didn't have money to spare but were also disdainful of the posing and anyway, we had cameras of our own.

Sometime during that introductory walk about with one friend or another we came on the ruin field of the Agora, the ancient large open place of assembly. I was very pleased to find that a reconstruction of the Stoa was underway, sponsored by the American School of Classical Studies, under supervision of the Greek governmental Department of Restoration – it says so in the diary. This was a colonnaded space on the side of an open gathering place, for merchants or artists to spread their offerings or for religious practises, rather like what I have seen in the centres of countless Latin American towns. Stalks of marble were being scaled down into round columns: a successive rough working down of courses close up to the desired circumference, they were then brought to perfect roundness, with progressively finer chisels. "The product, white and new, is a noble thing."

Alfred H. Siemens

I got into a 'discussion' with the workers, they in their English and I in my Greek. Naturally they asked about wages in Canada, and passed my astonishing answer along. I realized later I had probably contributed to discontent. Years after I had come and gone the new Stoa was in place.[56]

119

I would see the Parthenon in various lights: in the warm light of late afternoon against black clouds, in the moonlight, the marble glowing, at dawn as well, with a morning star over it. Here it's spot lit at night and me without a tripod.

The temple that impressed me most was that of Zeus, begun in Greek times and finished six hundred plus years later by the Romans.[57] It was huge, the basic lines are still sharp and true, and the capitals are Corinthian. I did a drawing of the fallen column, but it's lost and perhaps that's just as well.

Alfred H. Siemens

A grubby excursion

In the afternoon of the second day of saunter, the tempo changed; in the remaining time I would go on several excursions out of Athens, there were days of recuperation from these excursions, more new friendships, some good meals, further observations and ruminations. My daily rounds to the places where my money might be sent became increasingly irritating and finally infuriating, right up to a dramatic resolution.

In the meantime, I was off to Crete, apparently I needed to search out some roots of Greek culture. On this boat trip there was no bunk in a cabin and no restaurant as on the boat between Brindisi and Piraeus. I was going deck class. If they could do it, so could I. On the dock vendors and farewells, a din of Greek, donkeys pulling in carts, a paddy-wagon bringing convicts; they and their police escorts were coming with us.

On deck we soon heard music, as we had on the steamer through the Gulf of Corinth; a violinist offered folk tunes and others sang in response. The harmony was strange to me, the phrases seemed incomplete and unsatisfying. And there was dancing too, it went on and on. We were all swept along, occasionally there was applause. Some folk costumes were noticeable among the men: a rolled turban, breeches pleated over the crotch, waistcoats and boots – from who knew what rural place. Soldiers, like big children, eyed the foreigner with bland curiosity and asked 'English'? The prisoners were right there amongst us, handcuffed, sometimes arguing loudly and bitterly, their police guards quite inured.

"As night fell, silence slowly … settled upon the deck." Outside a cold wind whipped about, so people huddled into the lee of partitions. Everyone wore heavy clothes and most, like myself, had not bathed for some time, so we all smelled. Jokes here and there, sighs, remonstrances. Some toothless ladies in black laughed infectiously. I remember clearly that I was stretched out back to back with a burly guy on a hatch cover. In dim whoosiness I "thought of home scenes and the girl I might someday marry, as yet an anonymity, largely, but I was not depressed."

In the morning an ache began in my stomach, it rose to where I was perspiring all over and then just held, without letting up. The boat was docking, I couldn't stand and I didn't know how I would get off, but I did and sank down on some grass against a wall. Sheep were grazing nearby and passersby gave me long looks and the pain continued. I had to do something, so I slowly got up and made my way to the guards at the gate of the harbour. They sent for the police, an officer sat me down and began to massage my calves, hard, painfully hard.

Only once after that has anything similar happened to me. I was on a photo flight over the Tuxtla Mountains in Mexico, sitting next to the open door of a Cessna, gathering images for the book on the region of Los Tuxtlas. Tim Lapage was piloting and José Luis Blanco, my very good friend, was riding with us in the front right seat. I developed a severe stomach ache and feared I was about to explode. We were roughly equidistant between two airports, Tim had scanned the horizon for illicit drug strips, dropped down over the beach but found it littered with tree trunks; the nearby roads were too obstructed. We would just have to fly the forty minutes needed to get to Veracruz. I flattened a plastic bag under my butt. Then José Luis reached back for my hand and began to massage the heel of my thumb, hard, so hard that later his own fingers were raw. My gut subsided and we made it to Veracruz.

So there at the gatehouse of the port of Heraklion on Crete my pain subsided. In my diary it was beneficent divine intervention; I've since thought it must have been pain transference, or just distraction. I was given to understand that the boat on which I had come would leave again later that day and not be back for another three days, which I was sure I didn't have. I had come to see the archaeological site of Knossos, to savour something of the precursors of the Greeks, i.e. the Minoans. I would have to do it in a few hours, stomach unease or no, and I did.

I noted the Venetian fort,[58] out of the early thirteenth century, which pleases me now, having recently read the palatable bits out of Peter Ackroyd's biography of Venice.[59] The Venetians evidently bought Heraklion, settled their own people there, developed and controlled it as part of their farflung trading network and furthered its intellectual life, as well.

Alfred H. Siemens

Warm and fragrant spring air blew in at the open windows of the bus headed for Knossos; I was noting the elements of the rural landscape, building up my repertoire of impressions of the circum-Mediterranean world. In the spring of 2016, I was still at it, on a ramble with Alice through northeastern Spain, appreciating farmhouses and hilltop castles.

The archaeological site of Knossos represents the Minoan civilization, dating from the twenty-seventh to the fifteenth centuries BCE. The excavation is linked to a strong Indiana Jones-type personality and the reconstruction has been controversial, as I imagine in just about any other of the large excavated sites around the world. Its structure is highly complex, the setting beautifully green; it has yielded vast arrays of artefacts and images. The mural of the sport of bull-leaping[60] and the reconstructed corner of the palace, held up by tapered pillars originally of wood, are often taken to represent the genius of the culture.

Returning to Athens, the ship coasted westward, the wind fresh and the sea just about as blue as a Mediterranean sea should be. A squadron of dolphins escorted the ship for a while, then we put in at Rethymnon. My first minarets! On to Souda Bay; I had a quiet supper in the shade out on a sidewalk. There was music, the food was good; as elsewhere in Greece one went to the kitchen and pointed to appealing pans. Later I walked down the street. Solitude in the midst of whatever; I have always valued such time.

Then unwanted companionship intruded: a sailor and eventually a few of his friends. I was aware of having been brusque in earlier contacts with locals, and decided this time to enter into a conversation. My bare courtesy was taken as great friendship, and I was compromised until next morning.

Back on board again, I found myself carousing but without abandon, singing with arms slung about shoulders, but not liking the music. I imagined the folks at home seeing and misreading such a scene. No question of actually getting drunk, nor of sleeping; someone had lent me a blanket, but there was no place but the dirty floor.

In the diary I wrote "indescribable." Reading that I recognized an evasion. When I let the scene develop in memory I can see chickens roosting just over the approach to the little bar on deck, one had to step over their droppings to get morning tea.

On shore in Piraeus the forced camaraderie could finally end with a pose in front of a street photographer. He fussed about a rickety camera on a tripod, exposed the film by taking the lens cap off and putting it back on. Then he reached into the box through a long black sleeve, developed the image in a tray of solution inside and stabilized it in a pail of another solution outside. There I had it, "something between a positive and a negative". Unfortunately it's been lost.

Intimations of Byzantium in Athens

After Crete and some recuperation I tried again for a street wander. I had thought I might "linger at a garden bench to breathe scented evening air" but soon picked up very different impressions. An open-air meat market, strong lights, sellers out-shouting each other, chunks being carved off hanging carcasses on demand. I ducked into a church, as I had often done in Italy for quiet and meditation; this turned out to be Greek Orthodox with a service in progress. I had seen some sloppy Roman Catholic services but nothing like this. "Several singers were liturgizing, together and by turns. Occasionally a priest would appear at the portal of the sanctuary, after looking about, scratching himself and rearranging his drapes, he would more or less solemnly proclaim something." People in the back were in conversation, and this was a small place. Candle sellers were running what seemed to this idealistic young man a pretty sharp business: selling a candle, watching the buyer pray and leave, then snatching it out of its holder for melting down and resale. My awareness of Orthodoxy would evolve over the years and shift from disgust at its "calcified religious arteries" to something approaching admiration, to enthusiasm, for its music at least.

Christianity divided into western and eastern branches in the fifth century, the one centred on Rome and the other on Byzantium/Constantinople/Istanbul. The branching continued in the west and the east, of course, what I was seeing was the Greek version of Eastern Orthodoxy.

Golden-hued churches like the Panaghia Kapnikarea, the Church of Saint Mary, are embedded as islands in the street plan of the city. They date to the eleventh and twelfth century, and are very pleasing externally, but to a western Christian, they seem compartmentalized internally. The equal-armed cross plan doesn't facilitate focus; we are accustomed to a long nave and rites that climax at an altar, or perhaps at a pulpit on one side. Here there are lots of nooks and crannies, many mosaics, and icons everywhere. I found icon-kissing revolting; the icons themselves, thank you again Professor Binning, were quite attractive, highly stylized and mysterious, the precursors of Renaissance art.

Greek Orthodoxy runs on the Julian rather than our western Gregorian calendar. There would be a protestant Easter Sunrise service across from the Acropolis on April 10th and then the Orthodox loaves, eggs and worship at midnight in a small town a week later.

Mother had told us many times of her memorable visit to an Orthodox church in Moscow, as they were on their way from the Ukraine to Canada in 1926. Alice and I relived her visit in a monastery church in Kiev in 2004. The service is meant to recreate heaven, I've been told. Male harmonies, low basses, high tenors, sustained phrases, chants, solos and descants, fervent appeals for God to have mercy and curiously attenuated Halelu-u-jas. I have this music on CD's in my van; it has often taken me across town.

Somewhere in my schooling I had been made aware of Keats' Ode to a Grecian Urn.[61] It's heavily annotated in my English survey text as well, to which I have referred in my 'Preliminaries'. There were whole rooms of urns at the Archaeological Museum in Athens. The bulbous shapes are wonderfully graceful; I was particularly moved by what had been fixed in the glazes: the gods and maidens, the many folk that would not return to the town from which they had come, that would strain in racing competitions, cringe, love, or mourn forever. My favorite lines: 'Ah, happy, happy boughs! that cannot shed your leaves, nor ever bid the Spring adieu.'

Onto the Peninsula, just

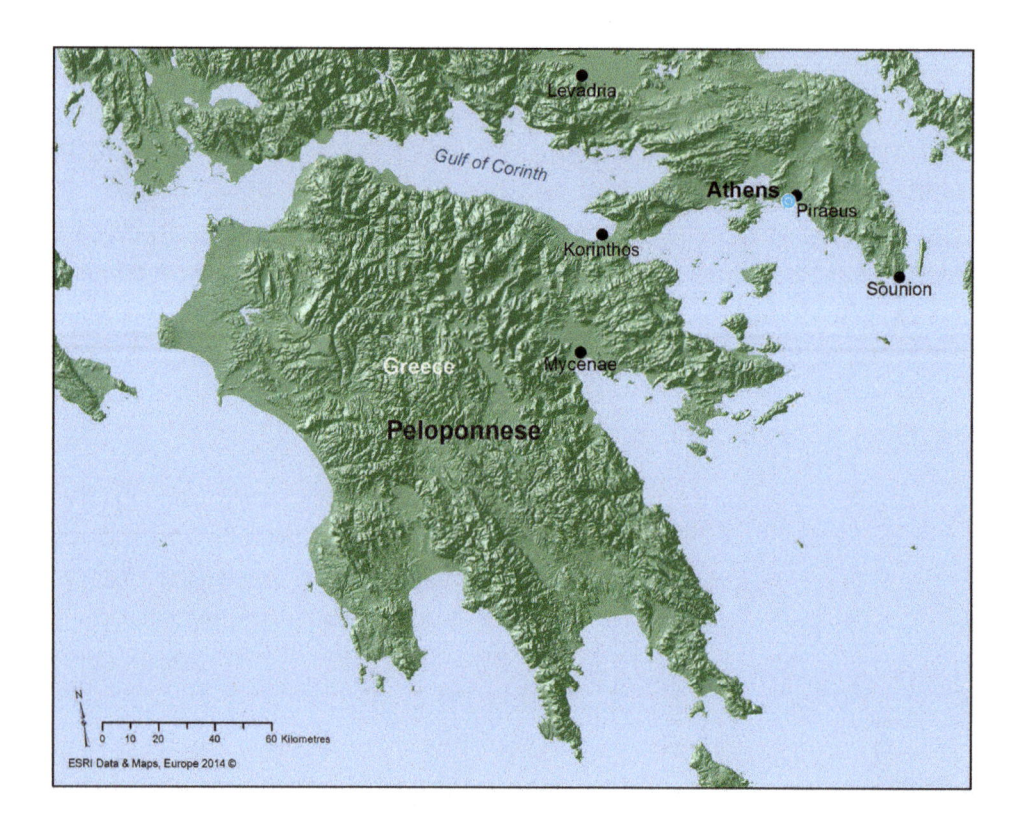

The daily checks at the post office and some bank or another where I had hopes my money would be sent to had become thoroughly tiresome. I was angry, my fists were clenched, but I didn't swear, at least not in the diary. I went to American Express and wired for money out of my own account – the fastest way of moving money at the time. I would still not get it until ten days later. I had to get out of Athens for a while. For some reason, no doubt on the basis of information in my guidebook , I fixed on the Peloponnesian Peninsula, west of Athens, and especially Corinth, or Korinthos, as a promising destination. I grabbed some essentials and left, hitch-hiking. "I cared not how or when I got there". But I was not so disgusted either; I stopped at Daphni, just outside of Athens, for its Monastery church and mosaic of Christ the Almighty, the 'Pantocrator.'[62] In the vast ruin field of Eleusis nearby I focussed not on the stones but on the flowers. I like that.

Green Mackinaw

Byzantine dome mosaic of Christ Pantocrator. *Public domain.*

128

The disgruntled exit from Athens turned into an idyll, with a bit of a digestive subtext. Hitch-hiking, I was picked up by Stamos, an educated man of the land, in his open jeep. He invited me to his farm, which became my base for two days of rambling around Corinth. How could one doubt that this was divine leading beyond any personal merit? Multiplied over and over, such would be the raw material for my inspirational talks of one kind and another when I got home.

All around was the Mediterranean rural landscape, "fresh and fragrant" from my perch in the open jeep. We stopped en route to buy a wheel of heavy bread and Stamos just threw it down on the floor. That's a way to treat bread? We would eat of it that evening. After we had turned into an impressive gate there were lemon and orange trees all around.

There was still time before supper so he took me into Corinth to see the Temple of Apollo, with which, I explained, I had strong associations. I had looked at pictures of it often, its stout columns and Doric capitals symbolized early Greece for me. But the light was not good, hence no photograph, only an appreciative look. Here, after fifty-six years, I have an image.[63]

Still before supper, I walked out with the hired man, talking in single words and gestures, among boughs weighed down with fruit, some of which he pressed on me, and which I ate right there. The sun broke out just before setting and turned everything gold.

I found myself in a warm home with thoughtful, English-speaking people. We ranged over many topics, including the antiquated agricultural methods in the surroundings and Stamos's efforts at modernization. Supper was mainly eggs fried in olive oil – after my appetizer of raw oranges. The diary slides euphemistically over what followed; I remember it very clearly. I was put into a fine bed in a room upstairs; the bathroom was on the ground floor. When I was hit by what I will call Corinthian Cramp I had to negotiate the creaking stairs of a sleeping house. On my way down I saw out of a large window that the sky had cleared; bright moonlight silvered the landscape and set off a slender cypress.

From the Stamos house I continued after some of the other antecedents of the art and architecture that I had seen in Athens, particularly the ruins of the ancient city-state of Mycenae, circa 1900–1100 BCE, which had come after the Minoans of Knossos on Crete. Mycenae's showpiece, the Gate of the Lions, was inaccessible, obscured by scaffolding and in poor light. I can remedy that now.[64]

At some time in high school I had brushed up against Euripides' play Electra and knew of Agamemnon and Clytemnestra. This was their country, I was following my guidebook industriously, making notes and even drawing diagrams of ruins related to these famous figures when dysentery hit me again and in desperation I had to resort to a furrow in a farmer's newly ploughed field.

I was determined to clamber up the castle (Akro Corinth) south of the city of Corinth, counting every drachma, walking up rather than taking a kid's donkey, even though he had already lowered his price. From among the walls of the old fortification there were great views in all directions, of course, including north-westward, over the densely settled northern shore of Peloponnesus and the Gulf of Corinth through which I had come on the steamer from Brindisi.

Alfred H. Siemens

And here things got really soulful, it being the run-up to Easter and all. Sheep, shepherds, tinkling bells, even a flute from somewhere, so, of course, on cue, there came as well the very familiar hymn from the VCF hymnal:

"All in the April evening,
April airs were abroad;
I saw the sheep with their lambs,
And thought on the Lamb of God."

Finding the sheep in my store of images and the hymn's stanza written out in my diary I am back in a VCF hymn-sing, sharing the hymnal with a neighbor, singing along with a will in whatever part seemed congenial, responding to somebody's vigorous conducting, appropriating the words. More, it is Sunday at the Wright mansion in Shaughnessy, where we met regularly for Bible Study. I'm in charge, preparing in a side room to go on. The group is singing in the adjacent assembly room; I can hear the sound through the wall now, hearty and joyous. These songs were part of my buoyant mind-set, part of what made 1954–55 a good year.

Waiting for a bus to Corinth in a little village near the ruins of the fortress, I was astonished again by the kindness of rural people, as in Puglia. Someone brought me a chair to wait on. The local bus agent came to give me information and help me to a ticket. "Passing school children greeted politely! I just nodded and smiled." Donkeys passed by; when one of them brayed I realized the irony of 'Sweetly sings the donkey at the break of day'. I looked at the worn shoes and poorly fitting threadbare clothes of people passing by, army surplus much in evidence. The faces of the older people were deeply lined. Times had clearly been hard and still were hard. Histories and novels out of the eastern Mediterranean would fill this out for me in later years.

Oliver

On the bus back into Athens, there happened to be a group of Brits including this immensely personable Oxonian, a member of their equivalent of Inter-varsity Christian Fellowship. I had been impressed by their prayer meeting some months past. We immediately connected, here was friendship of a high order, i.e. 'fellowship', an intensive interaction on the basis of shared ideas regarding spiritual experiences, not to mention my already considerable Anglophilia. This was all immensely reassuring during the conflicted last days in Athens but is just a bit embarrassing now – for the spiritual intensity and the penury.

Soon after we arrived back in Athens the two of us went on a day-trip to Sounion, particularly to see the Temple of Poseidon. Oliver was paying, as he would repeatedly in the days ahead. We almost missed the bus because of a student riot in Athens, supporting the annexation of Cyprus: hysteria, clubbing, arrests around the University Club.

Then it was April 10th, western Christianity's Easter. Somehow a group of four developed; Oliver, two other friends and I went for a sunrise service on Mars Hill, opposite the Acropolis. The morning star stood over the temples when we arrived. The service was mediocre, certainly in comparison to the earnest exchanges I was having with Oliver. Tourists around us were harnessed up "ready to shoot at the quiver of a meter needle." Inevitably we thought of the visit of St. Paul to Athens, as recounted in the book of Acts, and here in my study I remember how I first became aware of the story. In our home in Namaka there was a mauve hard-cover edition of a rather fine collection of etchings of biblical scenes. I pored over it as a youngster:

faces, gestures, clothing and backgrounds were apparently pressed into my memory. When I found a copy recently I was delighted, the pictures were familiar.[65]

St. Paul is preaching to the Athenians on Mars Hill, at some length, expounding on the idea that 'God that made the world and all things therein, seeing that he is Lord of heaven and earth, dwelleth not in temples made with hands.' Acts 17:22. OK.

A crazy final Athenian week

On Monday of this final week, "after I had had a delicious breakfast for about ten cents I had approximately eight cents left ... yet I was not perturbed." I soon had to accept another gift from Oliver. Also, good student that he was, he had somehow parlayed a fortunate contact into a good lunch in a home for the both of us.

'Student' equalled 'poor', you appreciated anyone who understood the exigencies and promise of being a student. You were on the lookout for cheap seats at concerts, cheap bus fares; you avidly exchanged information on the best deals on places to bed down, you 'scored' a nice lunch or hauled dried bread, some halvah and an orange out of a backpack. You walked wherever, scribbled notes, hitch-hiked, took pride in or at least overlooked scruffiness, arguing this or that point all the while with whoever was alongside.

Oliver was leaving on his own excursion to Crete, so I went to see him off in Piraeus. There was bedlam on the dock, hawkers, officers of the ship, travellers crowding aboard. Along came a new two-ton truck, just the cab and chassis, which had to be lifted up on to the deck. The block and tackle of a rickety crane swung over the heads of onlookers and then was finally fastened to the truck. For some sickening moments it hung at a crazy angle over us all. A man opposite me looked up with big-eyes and an open mouth. Finally the truck was swung around and brought down onto the deck with a thump. Minutes later the ship was off.

Every morning I did the "round" of Post Office, bank and American Express: nothing. Somehow I was able to maintain an equilibrium. I quoted a hymn in my diary and, rather melodramatically, a sentence out of the book of Job, as well: "Though he slay me, yet will I trust in him."

Honey coloured stone and an indigo sky provided me with the 'tah-dah' piece for my Grecian slide shows. When I got back to Hamburg the mother of the girl who wanted to be my girlfriend exclaimed, *"Wie Schön!"* At home I usually got a similar response. It was taken sometime during this last confused week in Athens. I remember reading the sky, recognizing the late afternoon potential for rich light and dramatic backdrop, and then racing in a taxi toward the Acropolis. I would race, and wait, for good light many times in the years ahead.

By Thursday I was antsy, next day was the eastern Good Friday, The American Express office, where I had initially wired for money out of my account at home, would be closed. Then there would be only one more day, Saturday, before my second Easter, with who knew what further delays.

In the late afternoon of Saturday it finally happened; the details are smudged in the diary but have been kept or perhaps made vivid in my mind by reason of the many retellings. Somehow I found that the money was receivable at a bank and it was almost closing time. An attendant was just bringing down the shutter on its front door. I grabbed the bottom bar with both hands. You can't, I gave him to understand. I want my money, and I got it. That's when I pinned one hundred American dollars into the frayed lining of my sports jacket with a safety pin, as in the story of Emil and the detectives that Mr. Thiessen had read us when we were in high school. I said my good-byes at the hostel and left town with Fred, an amiable companion in a good deal of my Grecian adventure.

SATURDAY, APRIL 16: BACK TOWARD HAMBURG

Another Easter

The first day hitch-hiking out of Athens got us as far as Levadia. It's a modest town, I've noted it on the map ten pages back. We had arrived on the night before Easter Sunday and there were no hotel rooms, there was not even room in the jail. However, the police invited us to spend the night in a wrecked 1950 Dodge off to the side of the town's square. The seats were still in good shape. But we didn't get much sleep since at midnight there was an intriguing service in the church with a veneration of special Easter bread and boiled eggs painted red. Bells and fireworks followed. Dubious 'resurrection soup' was served in a restaurant nearby but it actually was not bad at all. Yes, Resurrection Day, April 17; it would be very full and we would be very full too.

This picture was in my files, with useful notations on the back; I must have got it from Fred. He is the one with glasses in the back, I'm the one without glasses in the front. Our hosts are Jim and Alice Polymenacos. I don't remember how we met them, only that they were a very pleasant couple. They have taken us for a picnic on a mountain to the south of Levadia, which is just visible above our heads. We have lamb, woven Pascha or Easter bread and boiled eggs painted red, which we are cracking in a traditional way.

Back in town we noticed that families brought spitted lambs for roasting in cooperative rotisseries. When visitors wandered by they were offered slivers of roast lamb and a glass of Retzina, with probably a special Easter greeting too; we just couldn't understand it. Our parents had talked about Orthodox Easter day greetings in Russia when they were young: "Christ is risen. Yes, he is truly risen."

Gypsies plied the streets; their encampment was just out of town. Musicians made the rounds: clarinet, bouzouki, zither, playing music similar to what I had heard on shipboard going to Crete, the music I would come to enjoy when we all saw *Never on Sunday* a few years hence.

The 2nd Lieutenant of the town's police force took a liking to us, he invited us to a banquet of town dignitaries, with lots of army, and an oration by a priest. There was lamb, more Easter bread and boiled eggs, plus pastry and oranges, washed down with Retzina, another, kinder wine, and Ouzo, an anise-flavoured digestif.

Green Mackinaw

We were guests of the town, and a good feeling it was too. Would we please join the other men dancing in a line moving slowly around the square? Fred did quite well, I was a spectacle, wrapped still in old strictures.

138

Alfred H. Siemens

The 2nd Lieutenant and his very pleasant wife took us to their home as well. By this time we had eaten several times, but we ate more. A packed lunch was pressed on us and then our host took us out to flag a ride, without success. It seemed best to take a bus to a nearby railway station and then a train to Thessaloniki/Salonika. Climbing up into the railcar Fred fell and hurt his ankle; somehow I got him aboard and we reached Salonika, but his injury was disabling and he had to be taken to a hospital, where he was told he would need to stay two weeks. There went our companionable trip; I would need to go on alone.

Fingering the picture Fred had sent me I was beguiled once again by the thought of what might have happened to friends of long ago. I had followed up Goeff Hurley, my fellow M.A. student at UBC, but when I had his website in front of me I backed off, our life ways would probably be difficult to bridge. I contemplated searching for Oliver, but gave it up for roughly the same reason. Bob Detweiler had come up big and smiling on my monitor, but the picture was from an obituary. An affinity loosed by the Easter picnic picture, made me decide to try again, with Fred. He had been gruff sometimes, forceful, very sharp and certainly voluble, but sensitive too and thoroughly amiable. We were able to help each other. He had challenged me on various issues, like you didn't think there were red-headed and fair-skinned Jews, did you? He didn't share my religiosity, but apparently could tolerate it.

So I wrote by snail-mail, a business address was all the information I had, and not many days later I heard his voice on the phone. He was calling from New York, where he had become a well-established lawyer specializing in motion picture and television law. An animated conversation followed, and several more exchanges after that – two geezers happily reminiscing, falling into each other's sentences with elaborations and qualifications. He volunteered that meeting me was his first encounter with a born-again Christian, someone with integrity, who didn't press his views, but was prepared to discuss them. He looked back on his year in Europe with great satisfaction, as I did. It had been a remarkable thing to do in our time and it had been pivotal in his life, as it had been in mine. These were corroborations, grist for my memoir's mill.

Approach to the Balkans

There was some crazy toing and froing for several days between Salonika and the Yugoslavian border as I arranged money, visa and a ticket on a train, not just any train but one that would retrace part of the Orient-Express route; it was to take me to Vienna.

How to get the telling bits and a flow out of such days? Somewhere in my illustrious teaching career at UBC I freed up time for a course on film production. In the section on editing we were given a reel of several dozen short takes of a woman opening a door, going through it and closing it. Make a plausible, snappy narrative! We soon realized that this was not easy and that there were many possibilities. Editing the short visual and textual 'takes' of 1954–55 to achieve an agreeable flow has been a similar challenge many times over. Here's my approach to the 'approach'.

It was difficult, first of all, for a young Canadian to understand what was so terribly important about the upcoming border of Greece with Yugoslavia. I had made an effort: on the recommendation of friends I had taken a course on Slavonic Studies at UBC. Prof. Rose, wonderfully emphatic and obviously quite wise, walked back and forth in the front of the room, lecturing us on the history of Eastern Europe, stopping occasionally to pull up his socks. I was fascinated, Poland was partitioned several times, patriots and poets came and went. I got a fairly good mark, but I didn't come out with any clear overview. By the time there was fission and fighting in the region in the 1990s and we had scrabbled for explanatory literature, the ethnic complexities and old hatreds were somewhat clearer but I had to admit that it remained very difficult for an outsider to understand the Balkans. I did get to Poland and Czechoslovakia in 2000 and then the Ukraine and Russia too in 2004.

The preparation for the crossing in 1955 sharpened my cynicism over bureaucracy and procedural paperwork. To this day I marvel at bank clerks, for instance, who can deal with forms all day and not go mad. I have always been contemptuous of border minions, of frowns and stampings; now that I'm retired I can be dismissive of questionnaires.

At one point I needed to spend a night in the border station itself. Before I settled down I thought I would go for a walk first, I looked behind me and a guard was running up raising dust and waving his arms; he took me back to an officer who curtly explained that this was a military zone and one didn't just walk about. OK. From somewhere I got a meal and a glass of purple wine, began to read and write. My sleeping bag was warm, but the bench was hard.

At the other end of this yo-yo play, in Salonika, I am pleased to note now, I mailed away remittances to creditors. I also visited Fred in hospital and had a very satisfying talk with him about spiritual things, the things uppermost in my mind. I found he had made friends among the nurses and was having a good time. One of them wanted very much to detain me, but I escaped.

Somehow, out on the street on that same day, I met Elias, who wanted to come to Canada. He poured out his complaints about his country: ridiculous wages, moral degeneracy, foreign aid dissipated by the rich, an unkind society, really. I must have interjected something about the Greeks who had treated me well, he protested that the friendliness to foreigners was superficial. His living quarters in his parents' home were cramped; he saw no hope. This amplified what I had already heard from young men in Italy; in the years ahead I would hear variations on the urgency of emigration from young Mexicans. It strengthened my admiring perspective on my own country but also laid the germ of a foreboding: How would we deal with the influx?

Exploration in Salonika was not neglected during these days of bureaucracy; I was able to maintain my sensitivity to the fortuitous tableau. These people were gracious enough, I assume, to let me make this composition. I couldn't really deal with the problem of strong contrast that the image presented until I had *PaintShop Pro* at my disposal half a century later. What did I confirm for these people? What would they be discussing later?

Once I was actually on my way northwestward people on the train were curious about me. I heard them identify the stranger as *"Americani"* or *"Germani"*. He studied maps and made notes. I wondered what they were saying about me. I was moved to be able to generate a conversation with a pleasant Greek couple in bits of German and English: verbs, nouns, personal pronouns and gestures. A smile and an 'ah' after a successful point made the conversation seem immensely worthwhile. They shared their Easter bread and eggs with me, and wanted to know about my father; a trip of this kind was inconceivable if there was not a rich, supportive father. I had to make them understand that my background was quite otherwise and that, in fact, my father was now an invalid.

I think now of what I had the carver put on my father's gravestone: "Sown in weakness, raised in power (I Corinthians 15:43)". This was a way of acknowledging carefully a bit of how things had been, of signaling my high regard for my father and remaining within the idiom of the Mennonite graveyard where he is buried. John was not strong in health; he was prone to depression. He wanted to sell but had to farm, first in Namaka, Alberta, and then in Abbotsford, B.C. For some years he was a rural mailman in Abbotsford, for which elderly people remember him still. He aspired to entrepreneurship but achieved it only once, when he managed a jewelry store in Vancouver. He didn't accumulate much, but he was warm and had integrity. For me he was strong, I am in his debt for much love, numerous fatherly assists, for help in making the decision to go to university and for encouragement to go and ask Alice to marry me. He did not leave a diary.

Then how had I got the money to make this grand tour? I explained that I had worked. How prosperous must be the country in which a student working could earn such a trip! I was convinced of that myself, but the many qualifications I would have liked to have made had to be left unsaid.

Substantial guard posts appeared as we approached the northern border of Greece, down in the bottom right corner of the map.[66] The uniforms of the guards were grey and their caps carried a red star on a white field.[67] This was ominous to the young man who had heard stories all his life about the menace of communism.

The railway stations were generally squalid and the tracks closely guarded, but over the cityscape of Skopje I noted minarets. I had first seen them on Crete, this was now the second intimation of Islam. I had wanted to see these symbols of the Near East since I was a kid. I got to appreciate them more fully in travel with Alice to Morocco in 2010, where I listened to antiphonal calls to prayer very early in the morning from our hotel above Fez. In 2013, I was able to photograph them in Istanbul.

Alfred H. Siemens

All of Tito's Yugoslavia passed by our train's windows in one day. For some security reason there was no getting off before Vienna. So I needed to 'read' landscapes with a will.

Agricultural fields and pastures were spread over the flatlands. The Prairie boy noticed there were no fences, but there were lone trees in the fields. I would eventually learn how in some long-settled European regions these trees have ritualistic importance. The villages were compact, as I had already seen them in Greece; rural settlement was very different from widely scattered farms of my childhood. In the mountains nearby villages were perched in defensible positions. Cereals were being grown on any amenable slopes, with orchards interspersed, and pastureland too, dotted with cattle and sheep. Oxen were drawing ploughs, men and women worked in the fields, the women in dark dresses and white shawls. All this would come to mind in later seminars on the nature of peasantry; we struggled with key indicators, definitions and comparisons. It's quite a problematical category.

Many slopes carried *maquis*, the dense low scrub forest that results from frequent burning over relatively arid land. This vegetation has long provided refuge, in folklore at least, for bandits and guerrillas. Beyond the maquis the mountain lands were mostly denuded. I was enlarging my appreciation of deforestation, a huge theme throughout the Mediterranean lands.

I got a whiff from urban signs of the shift to the Germanic as we went further westward. I would only begin to understand how culturally complicated these lands were, how deep the hatreds ran, when the world was confronted some years later with new Balkan wars.

At the Semmering Pass just south of Vienna the train halted; a Russian soldier appeared at the end of our carriage, looking just the way I had always imagined a Russian soldier should look: fur cap, round face, boots, belt and a huge gun, patrolling, intimidating.

Viennese Woods

There were Russian soldiers in the streets of Vienna too, easily recognizable in their brown uniforms. After the war, Austria had been divided into zones of occupation and Vienna happened to be in the Russian zone. Slogans had been mounted at intersections, as well as large hammers and sickles. The occupation would be over before the end of 1955.

The youth hostel was in the woods near the city, the "Wienerwald", the Vienna Woods. One immediately hears the old waltz. I lucked into a celebration of Scouts, who did a torchlight parade. Lines of wavering lights were mirrored in pools from a recent rain, there was a good deal of ceremony and vacuous speechifying, which unfortunately, unlike in Levadia, I could understand. Later I would find the torchlight parade had deep roots in the history of ritual, it was inaugural, celebratory, meant to animate, particularly at youth events, and particularly in Germanic Europe.

Alfred H. Siemens

The young romantic was thrilled. Over the years, this inclination has brought me pleasure but also embarrassment. One doesn't shuck such a tendency, one tries to express it judiciously, mostly cover it up. It's not conducive to being taken seriously at the university. It was a handicap and I wasn't always able to throttle it in time. Now I can afford to care less.

By the time I had followed the young man as far as Vienna I was thinking more and more of variations on a particular German word: *Stöber*. His diligence suggested it, his eager following up on cues in guidebooks and maps, his grasping of images. I especially like *aufstöbern*, meaning to search out, to track down and to rummage around in, quite like a hunting dog. The root can be used as a noun and qualified as needed.

'Kulturstöber'

Next morning I began my Viennese 'Kulturstöber'- my own determined pursuit of the beautiful and the significant in this venerable city. Countless young people have trailed through European museums, guidebooks in hand and with greater or lesser wonder; this was how I did it, how I firmed up aesthetic standards for my liberal arts education. I was slightly jaded after the Mediterranean lands, but soon regained my enthusiasm as I went at the paintings in the Kunsthistorisches Museum. I'm quite swept up in them again now, reminded of the marvellous emotional yields of the visits to great collections during that year and the years to come.

Maria Theresa (1717–1780), the Hapsburg "archduchess of Austria", mother of sixteen children, who ruled for forty years, sits between the two identical museums, the Naturhistorisches Museum and the Kunsthistorisches Museum and for the life of me I can't find out if this is the one or the other. It doesn't matter.

William Neufeld, one of our teachers at the Mennonite Educational Institute (MEI) in Abbotsford sparked something in me that led to the classes at UBC with B.C. Binning and a long involvement with art and with imagery. He got each of us in his art appreciation class a packet of reproductions of famous paintings. I'd like to make up a short set here from paintings seen during a morning at the Kunsthistorisches Museum as a kind of memorial to Mr. Neufeld. I can give them a visual richness that the high school packet never had.

Raphael's Madonna of the Meadow[68] has the colours that epitomize colour, the tantalizing landscapes in the background and of course the enigmatic face.

Of the various Rembrandt self-portraits in the museum, this mature, confident face, the unpretentious working get-up and the searching eyes appeal to me.[69]

Peter Paul Rubens' women sit, lounge and romp voluptuously through European museums until one mostly just passes them by; enough already. This one that I found in Vienna appeals to me now.[70] Nothing like it would have been in any packet Mr. Neufeld handed out to Mennonite high-schoolers.

Alfred H. Siemens

Ruisdael's Windmill[71], on the other hand, was in his packet, I remember being thrilled by it. The nature of the low country of northern continental Europe may well have been discussed in class; allusions were probably made to Mennonite history in this part of the world. It's a cool, windy day at Wijk in The Netherlands; sun and clouds conspire in a shifting spotlight.

In Vienna I also came on the Breughel mother lode. I have since been detained many times in front of one or another of the paintings by Pieter Breughel the Elder.[72] I have examined the detail area by area, as in this wintry scene, the leafless branches and the crows, the frozen lakes, the players on the ice, evocative details, such as the young woman pulling along an older one seated on a chair with runners.

In the museum there were "rooms and rooms of junk". I think I meant silverware and furniture, plus a quantum of "Classical stuff" says the guy who has just been to Rome and Athens, and "Egyptian things" including mummies "shelled and unshelled".

The 'Kulturstöber' continued in a neighbouring church for a Mozart mass in G major by the Vienna Boys Choir and the Hofburg orchestra: "An elaborate and carefully executed religious ceremony. The music, robes, incense, the ritual and chant made a unified work of art. "A subset of the choir was later trotted out for the visitors."

Alfred H. Siemens

At the Imperial Treasury, after noting crowns on red velvet under glass, jewels, robes and whatever, I thought of Grey's 'Elegy', and what has always been for me its key stanza:

"The boast of heraldry, the pomp of power/And all that beauty, all that wealth e'er gave/Awaits alike th' inevitable hour:/The paths of glory lead but to the grave."

There were other wonderful Viennese things in buildings around Maria Theresa's statue, including a collection of imperial coaches at the Wagenburg: sixty vehicles out of royal holdings and aristocratic estates, many of them as stylish as Rolls-Royces. [73]

Across the northern foothills of the Alps

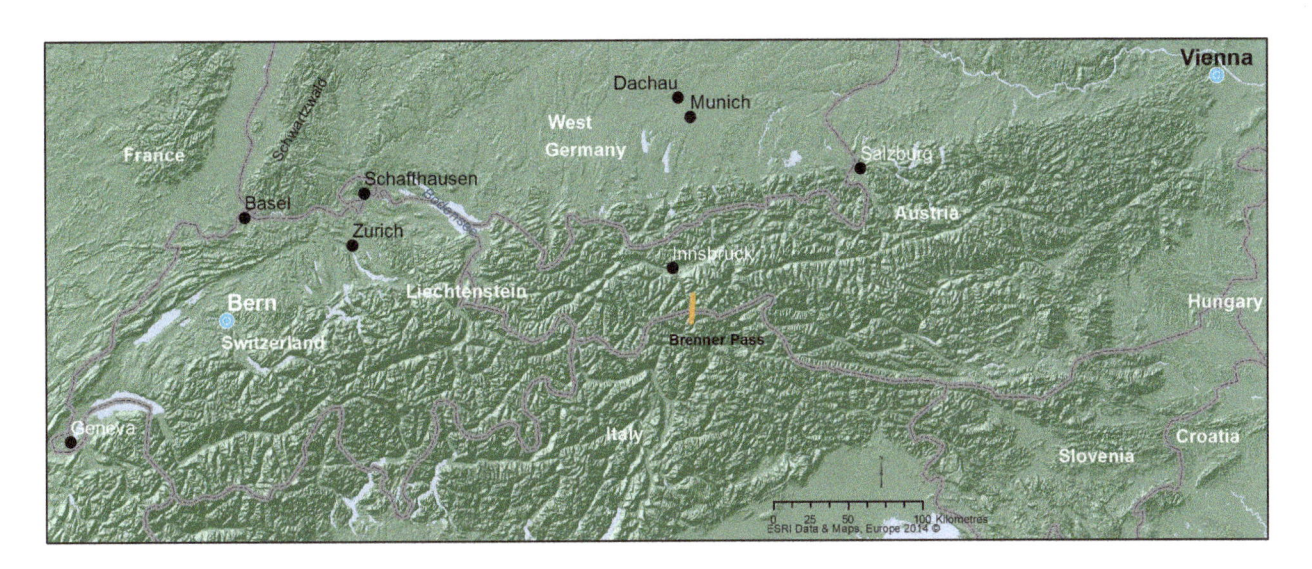

German geographers have a fine word for the band of landscapes that rise up southward toward the Alps, in Austria, Germany and Switzerland: *Alpenvorland*. This country attracted me, I felt well placed. I'm thinking of the weight that human geographers put on 'place,' implying a more than passing relationship between people and the landscapes in which they find themselves. It was early summer and the country around me felt much like home, like southwestern British Columbia, but manicured and culturally dressed. I have always felt southwest BC was built up rough and 2x4 ready: the mountain backdrop is glorious but the 'built environment' is mostly mediocre.

I suppose I had received a scholarship payment in Vienna, as arranged. And I was back in orderly Germanic lands, after all. But frugality was necessary still, I needed to stick to a daily limit of something like the equivalent at the time of CAD$1.50 a day.

In the hill land near the Alps it was potato-planting and manure-spreading time. I had some personal knowledge of this. That square can standing in the field was very like the one I had used every day at home in Abbotsford to carry chicken manure from under the roosts out to a berry field. By the time I got to graduate school in Wisconsin I had an appreciation of the wisdom of the European combination of crop and livestock farming. I would be alert to this issue when I got to reading about rural development problems in Latin America and was pleased when I saw manuring in the European immigrant enclaves in southern Brazil.

Alfred H. Siemens

On another rural walk near Salzburg with Elizabeth Neufeld, about whom more in a moment, I came up close to a cluttered farmyard where some boys were milking. All around were the implements needed to work on the land and care for animals; there were stored building materials plus junk here and there. A manure pile had pride of place in the front of the farmyard. Espaliered fruit trees grew against walls. A dwelling in chalet style anchored it all, signaling tradition and adaptation, with overhanging gable and balcony, ornamental woodwork and maybe some geraniums in boxes and lace curtains in upper windows.

I have always enjoyed rural clutter, visually and as a material compendium of the history of vernacular architecture and technology. In the Canadian Prairies and the Plains of the US I am always fascinated by the eddies of retired farm machinery somewhere outside of the farmstead's shelterbelt; there may well be the skeleton of a binder, maybe the forequarters of a wagon, the motor out of a truck, even a rusted single-shared horse-drawn plough hidden somewhere in the weeds, with which it all began. Trashy yards in Appalachia are a delight, in Baja California, anywhere.

In Austria it was early May, coming up to Mother's Day. I decided to bring her dried wild flowers framed under glass, including Edelweiss.[74] They were still there among my parents' memorabilia when it came time to box it all. I know my mother cherished them, they were from the time her son was reasonably understandable and explainable to her contemporaries.

My mother was a sensitive soul, with affinities for the Canadian Prairies even stronger than my own; she meticulously stitched flowers onto pillow cases. She often told us of a delightful youth in Russia, strong friendships and a most congenial home in what is now the southern Ukraine. In her nineteenth year she experienced the profound dislocation of immigration to Canada and always afterward felt thwarted, she had not been able to develop her abilities nor ever fully to express her sensibilities, which was what father felt as well. She had her flights of fancy, but remained earthy, devout and resourceful – she had to be, there was never much money. I owe her my romanticism, I think. I recall lots of cheerful times but also bitter talk of the hand she had been dealt.

Eva left a diary of the pivotal event of her life, the journey from Moscow to Manitoba, as well some subsequent musings which I found and reflected on.[75]

How many times does one get to do idyllic walks in upper Austria? Not often. Dark woods, chalets, perched towns and villages. I heard melodious brooks, an alphorn, yodelling and a cuckoo somewhere among the trees at dusk. I'm not making this up, it's all there in the diary. While rowing a boat on a quiet lake I realized I was unwinding now from the stresses of the latter parts of the Mediterranean trip.

I was staying in Puch near Salzburg[76] with Betty Neufeld, a relative. She was thoughtful, sensitive, spiritually as committed as I was, somewhat older, a counsellor therefore, serving as a missionary to children. We rushed into town for a concert: Bach's *Kunst der Fuge*, me in a roll neck sweater and army surplus pants, tired after rowing for an hour and hiking around in several towns, among long dresses in the concert hall foyer, dark suits and grey ties. I was respectful of the music, but not much more. I've become notorious in the family and among friends for daring to put down Bach, especially his relentless beat.

We had soulful exchanges – I'm being respectful. We told each other our personal histories, crises, concerns over friends and relatives. We both felt the imperative of proselytization strongly, the need for the revitalization of evangelical Christianity in Europe and the deepening of spirituality in our home churches. This paralleled exchanges I had had with Bob Detweiler, Helmut Funke, and Karl Sundermeier. Such was my spiritual context and my mindset at the time.

At Munich, in April of 1955, the journey southward toward the Mediterranean that I had begun in February, closed its loop. I picked up my stored moped and hoped to putter westward toward Basel, but its fuel line had been damaged in transit and I couldn't get out of town. Other problems developed with the tires. At one point I tried to inflate one of them myself, the attendant was shouting and waving. BANG. I had used a high pressure air hose suitable for truck tires. I was back and forth from repair shops, and considerably frustrated – on such days the orthography of the diary enlarges and becomes aggressive. Eventually the moped did facilitate the most exquisite landscape sensations of the whole journey.

Waiting for repairs I 'did' the Deutsches Museum, a museum of technology. A room of grand pianos, for instance and just then someone was going from one to the other trying them out. There was a locomotive and an Opel automobile sliced down the middle. I was brought up short by an inscription about Werner von Siemens, one of our famous antecedents, who invented the generator and founded the electrical and telecommunications company which everyone knows about. Hotel clerks in Latin America, or Africa, look up and ask "*That* famous name?" I tend to answer: 'Yes, but unfortunately I don't own any stock.'

When the moped was finally roadworthy I was off to Dachau, the concentration camp turned memorial. A Star of David rises over a huge mass grave. One passes by a 'corpse depot,' a gas chamber with a hole through which guards could look in to see if all were dead and ovens with horrible mouths. Only a very narrow tray is needed to hold a ravaged corpse! Nearby stand pokers and scrapers ... I left southwestward, puttering, and the mood shifted.

The rolling topography of Southern Germany was all around me again: pastures and cultivated fields, blooming apple trees and dandelions, nestled towns and villages, farmyards, i.e. '*Bauernhöfe*'. The breeze was in my face, it was haying time and I was glad to be alive. Years later I was pleased to hear my son talk about smelling the landscape as he and a friend were on a run with their 700cc road bikes somewhere in the western US.

I stopped for solitary picnics, got back on and just rolled it a bit until the motor kicked in. At one point I was singing loud enough to drown out the motor, thinking maybe the nonsense with the fuel line and the tires had been outweighed.

During all of my travels between Hamburg and Munich I looked for church spire signals: gabled or pointed spires in the north indicated Protestantism, gracious onion-domed spires in the south, Roman Catholicism. I was now in the Roman Catholic south, with its baroque churches, inspired by the Counter-Reformation. Thus were the faithful dazzled and those dissuaded who might have been tempted into the Reformation.

It's all represented well in the Wieskirche,[77] the church in the meadow, which is what the name means. The interior is exuberant, I'd already seen such an interior in Rome, in the Church of the Most Holy Name of Jesus, the mother church of the Society of Jesus: asymmetry, endless swirls, pastel colours and gold. Angelic figures leave their frames and gesticulate into the clouds. All is exaggeration, violent emotion, eyes are half-closed in trance or stupor. Photography was 'verboten' in these interiors, of course, so one had to search out representative images later, much later.

Green Mackinaw

Alfred H. Siemens

Eventually, in Latin America, I would come on the transposed Baroque, especially in Ecuador and in Mexico; in the latter an ultra-Baroque, called Churriguresque.[78] Much too much, the Protestant tends to think, it fairly invites ecstasy!

Castling

The word comes from chess. In Rome and Korinth I had begun appreciating castles. That continued here in the Southern Germany, and would go on eventually with Alice and the children in France, and then just the two of us in Spain. There's always the angled mass against the sky, a long gradual approach and an entry through a main gate. Maps and guidebooks to hand, with or without cameras. Again and again it's been a pleasure, appreciating placement, view and form, noting draftiness and hygienic arrangements, walking the walls, clambering down into storage rooms, reading the placards, and imagining the goings on.

Just west of the Bodensee, headed for my dip into Switzerland, I came on Hohentwiel,[79] perched on the remains of an old, hard volcanic core, its cliffed eminences ideal for fortification. It was a great day: budding trees, birds, a cuckoo in the distance – always great to hear that iconic intruder on other birds' nests.

Green Mackinaw

Alfred H. Siemens

Schloss Neu Schwanstein is in the same region: kitsch supreme, an inspiration, apparently, for Walt Disney. I quite enjoyed it. This almost unbearably picturesque little residence was built by Ludwig II of Bavaria in the nineteenth century as a pure and utter personal indulgence. It was intended to be a theatrical interpretation of the Middle Ages. Wagner was his friend, themes out of operas are painted on various walls. The great hall could accommodate duelling singer ensembles, fine decorations and furniture right and left. The troubling and intriguing basic thought is that Ludwig lived here for less than half a year before he was drowned in a nearby lake. Several years later the castle was declared a museum; everything still looks new, the utensils in the kitchen are unbattered and the walls clean. From out of the balcony windows on the left the meaning of *Alpenvorland* is clear: hill land leading up into the mountains.[80]

A particular bell

This quite ordinary-looking bell was poured in 1486, it hung till 1895 in the tower of the Münster at Schaffhausen. The band at the top is inscribed: "*Die Lebenden rufe ich, die Toten beklage ich, die Blitze breche ich*" - I call the living, mourn the dead and stop lightning.

Evidently this bell inspired Schiller's long poem, *Das Lied von der Glocke*, which might be translated as *The Ballad of the Bell*. It was introduced into the 1945–46 curriculum of the MEI by Mr. Thiessen, he of the story of Emil and of the speaking choir. The ballad was a felicitous introduction, without a doubt. It fostered all sorts of edifying sentiments about the stages of human life, enlarged our exposure to good German and some poignant poetry, which did not prevent us from flinging bits of it about the schoolyard as irreverent epithets.

The bell sits now in a quiet courtyard in Schaffhausen, I paused there a while and recited what I remembered of the poem. When I googled the poem I found I recognized many passages clearly, as well as the gist of the whole. In our school annual of 1945–46 there is a commemorative montage of fuzzy photos. We not only memorized the poem, but also sang the musical version and put on tableaux: '*lebende Bilder*'.

Alfred H. Siemens

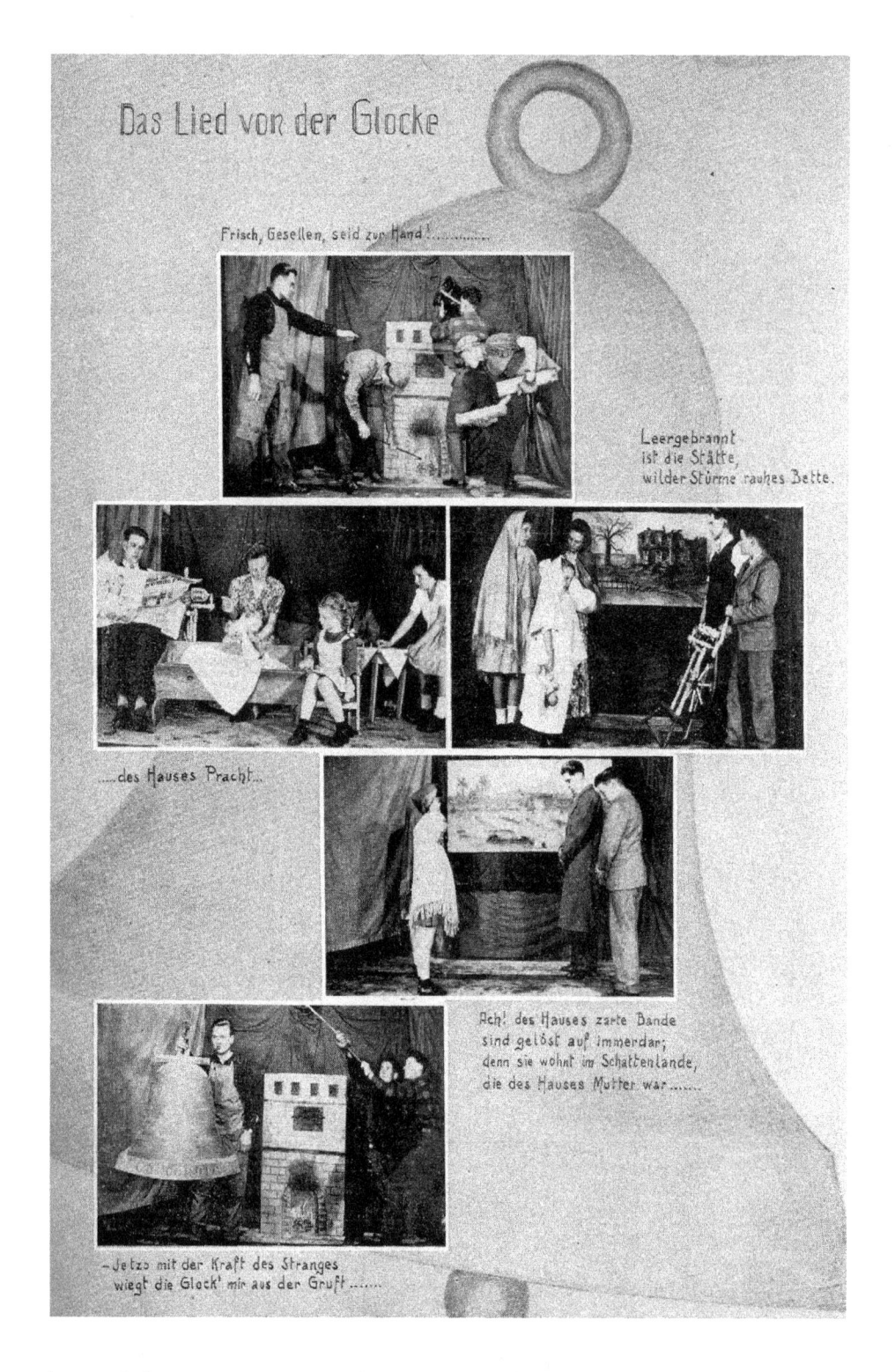

Lorna is long gone, Henry too, George? Lena? Bless them.

Near the end of the ballad a rope is pulled taut, the new bell moves free of its form and then swings free: *"Sie bewegt sich, schwebt"*. Makes me think again of the sensation of a train coming away from the platform in Hamburg's *Dammtor Bahnhof*, a hot air balloon or a helicopter leaving the ground.

Deviation

I needed to veer off southward into Switzerland to drop off the exposed Ektachrome film that I had rolled from a bulk roll into individual canisters before departure. It was to go to a lab near Zürich, which was the only place on the continent where it could be developed. It also seemed necessary to hurry, I was already late for the beginning of the next semester in Hamburg, so I stored my slow and wilful moped in Schaffhausen and continued southward by thumb and rail.

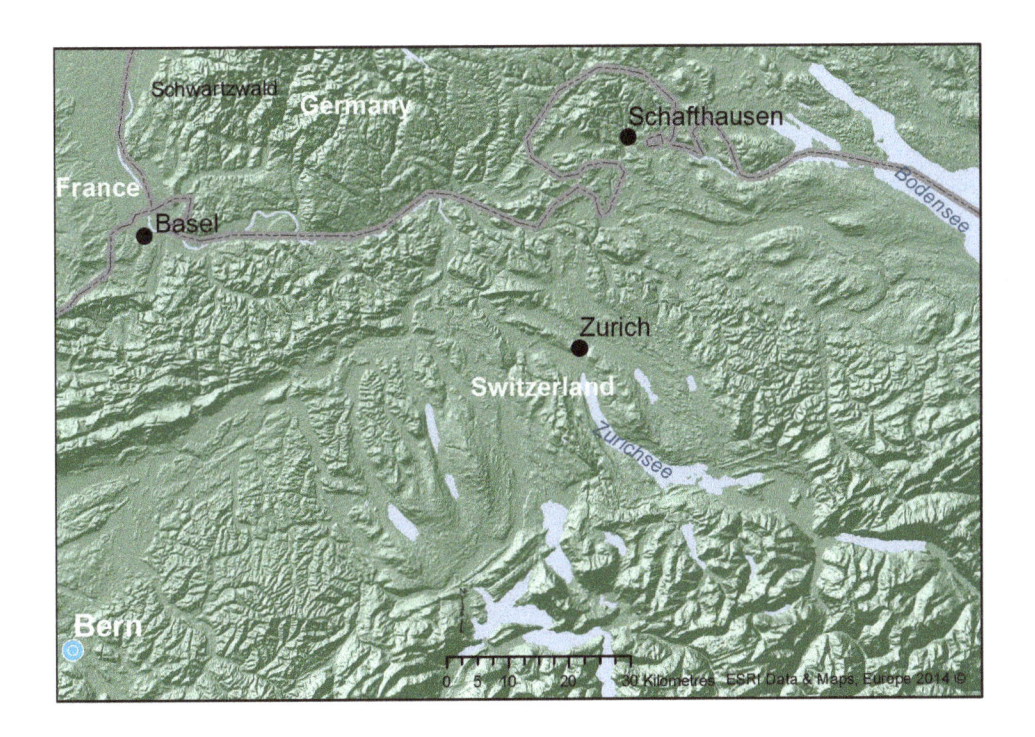

But I kept up the *Stöber*. One couldn't pass up the Landesmuseum in Zürich, a vast repository of alpine material culture. In the diary I zeroed in on particular fascinations, such as a collection of bells, with a little hammer hung nearby with which to make them ring.

More importantly, there were table-top models of *Pfahlbauten*. These were prehistoric dwellings built on pilings in shallow water from 3000 to 1800 B.C. on the Zürichsee, a lake near the city. A reconstruction of such a settlement can now be seen on the shore of the Bodensee, a lake to the northeast of Zürich.[81] It was my first real visualization of an ancient way of living on the margins of wetlands and I would keep this old world analogue in mind when in the 1960s I began investigating wetland margins in Mesoamerica for evidence of ancient settlement and agriculture.

Jim Draper

We met in a youth hostel in Switzerland, a friendship developed, a bond with long-term practical consequences. The image is mid 1970s and we are on the farm south of Cultus Lake in British Columbia that Jim, my brother-in-law Walter Bartsch, and I owned jointly. On my right is Jim, on my left, Jim's daughters from his first marriage, Maria and Diana, Jim's third wife, whose name has escaped us, our Howard, futzing about with something, then Alice, our Yvonne and Barbara.

I met Jim just after I had left the moped in Schaffhausen and began hitchhiking to have the films developed near Zürich. I liked him immediately, he was gracious, but self-possessed too, not religiously inclined, yet obviously prepared to be a friend to a zealous Christian. He remained a friend after my Christianity had faded and on through to his own passing in 2004.

Various details stick: he introduced me to little blocks of instant oatmeal, just right for efficient, healthy travel. He interested me with his account of his travel in 1953 from Capetown to Cairo and his work in combatting a plague of locusts. He had studied at UBC and on return from Europe he would go to the University of Wisconsin where he did his PhD, as I did, but along a very different path: he focussed on adult education. The University of Toronto became his university, and India became his *locus operandi*, his passion, as Mexico became mine.

We shared an appreciation of the aesthetics of rurality. Somehow, and I don't recall just when, he raised the importance of the purchase of land, now, while we were young, putting such money as we could scrape together into a partnership, not just or even primarily as an investment, but as a way of securing an attractive place for us and our eventual families to spend holidays. This firmed up my own ideas and stimulated me to head up the three- way partnership for the purchase of a sixty-acre farm south of Cultus Lake. My family, Walter's family, our relatives and friends would become the main immediate beneficiaries of this purchase; Jim was by now mostly between Toronto and India, seldom in B.C. But on that one day his family and mine were together in that lush grass.

Jim, Walter and I had bought the farm from John Minarech, of Czech background, who homesteaded here in the 1930s. He cleared the land piece by piece, split cedar trees for boards and shingles, built the house and barn and everything else on the place. He smoked meat, canned fruits and vegetables, worked away all of his mature adult life here on this farm, something like thirty years. When we met him he was alone, estranged from his family, cantankerous his neighbours said, in hostile surroundings he said. But his strength was giving out, he had to sell. Here were these urbanites who wanted his land, whom he could not credit for a while, but after four weekend negotiating visits we came to terms. Two views of rurality met, he saw hard work and relentless economic constraints; we were thinking aesthetics, recreation – and long-term investment. The greyed and aging buildings represented his life's work. I was never able to forget that; here's to him. For years we rented out the land for grazing but were eventually forced to sell the whole farm to the army. They wanted to establish a shooting range, an outlier of the Chilliwack armed forces base, but that never materialized.

Alfred H. Siemens

I always did quite a number on Appalachia in my lectures on the Cultural Geography of North America and knew very well that our neighbours in this valley had been called B.C.'s hillbillies. It was recreation to assume such a role, to shoot at targets with my .22-calibre rifle and then range freely with my cameras, finding spiritual escape from the exigencies of academic life and create images, as in this superimposition that found its way on to the cover. An apple still hanging late in the year became a black moon.

Our children and their cousins vividly recall 'spook walks.' I would take all the pre-teens, Walter's Sonia, Rick, Carla and Bruce, the children of Amanda, Alice's sister, as well as our Yvonne, Barbara and Howard into the forest at night, without lights. I wish Jim's children could have been with us too, at least once. Wonderful skitterings and screaming!

Jim and I spent several days together in Switzerland. Both of us were taken with Zwingli outside of the Water Church in Zürich. The exploration and refinement of this image here now has made me wonder. The Bible in hand yes, but the sword? I did some digging, as I have done often during this whole venture, and there he is, a contemporary of Erasmus, a reformer who anticipated Luther in some respects and would eventually be at odds with him.[82] He was incensed by the laxity of Roman Catholic clergy and the sale of indulgences, he advocated changes in the ritual, he debated forcefully and preached, and he fought physically for all this too. The fledgling Anabaptist movement in the region was more radical than he was so he persecuted them mercilessly.

That sword was useful to him. What was Jim making of all this and of me? Did he leave a diary, I wonder?

Jim and I walked for many kilometres, I don't remember exactly why, but it was partly about saving money and partly about just enjoying the landscapes. We had a fine moon one evening, a fresh, scented morning next day, birdsong as I stopped somewhere to write in the diary. We passed among alpine farmsteads: stained wood on stone foundations cantilevered out on amazing slopes, clutter under spacious eves, vines reaching into carved gables.

'Die grosse Dummheit'

I don't need to translate that, do I? Jim was with me, and very supportive too, when I blundered rather drastically. The main visual yield of my European travels to that point was a rattle of film canisters in a little green sack. I left it on the seat beside me when Jim and I got out of a ride, thanked the man and waved to him as he drove off.

I cringe in recollection, nothing, well almost nothing, is as bad as the loss of exposed film. Cold anger collected in my guts, anger at my own lapse. This is corrosive, I know, but it happens. I reported it to the police and they began checking up and down my route for my films. Instead of daily checks at post offices and banks for money, I was now checking daily with the police from wherever I found myself.

And all the while yours truly was able to relegate anxiety and continue the Kulturstöber, some with Jim, some alone. There was a trip across the

Alfred H. Siemens

Vierwaldstättersee on the *Wilhelm Tell*, for heaven's sake, to the meadow where myth has it that late in the fifteenth century representatives of the cantons of Uri, Schwyz and Unterwalden met to swear an oath of unity against their oppressors, the "Rütlischwur," and thus laid the foundation for Switzerland. On one placard or another I remember reading that this was a legend. We had learned it by heart in high school as fact. I found that what with the introduction to Shiller's ballad, and the history of the hearth of Anabaptsism and thus of Mennonitism, we had actually been taught a good deal in the MEI about this European nexus.

Early the next day, the 7th of May, I was in a friendly police inspector's office, I can't say now just where. He made a call and then told me: *"Der Sack ist in Zürich."* My sack of films had been found and was being held for me. I'm thinking thanks to them again; their sympathetic and effective action still informs my view of their country. I could now quickly take care of all the practicalities regarding development – the finished images would be mailed to me – and head northward. There would be slides!

167

Sprint

It seemed important now to get back to the university, after all I was on a scholarship and nothing if not conscientious. There wasn't much of 1954–55 left. I feel I need to keep up the pace here in my account as well.

The moped was to take me through the *Schwarzwald*, The Black Forest, then down into the plain of the Rhine, northward to Heidelburg and Mainz. I would hitch-hike from there to Hamburg.

From the moped the Schwarzwald looked about like this:[83]

A 'Hochstrasse', or high road follows the ridges. Dense stands of conifers give the mountains a dark green that is almost black. They are dappled with clearings and webbed with roads and footpaths; solid stands of trees with roughly equal height fringe many ridges indicating successive harvesting and replanting. These forests have long been managed and the history of their exploitation is complex.

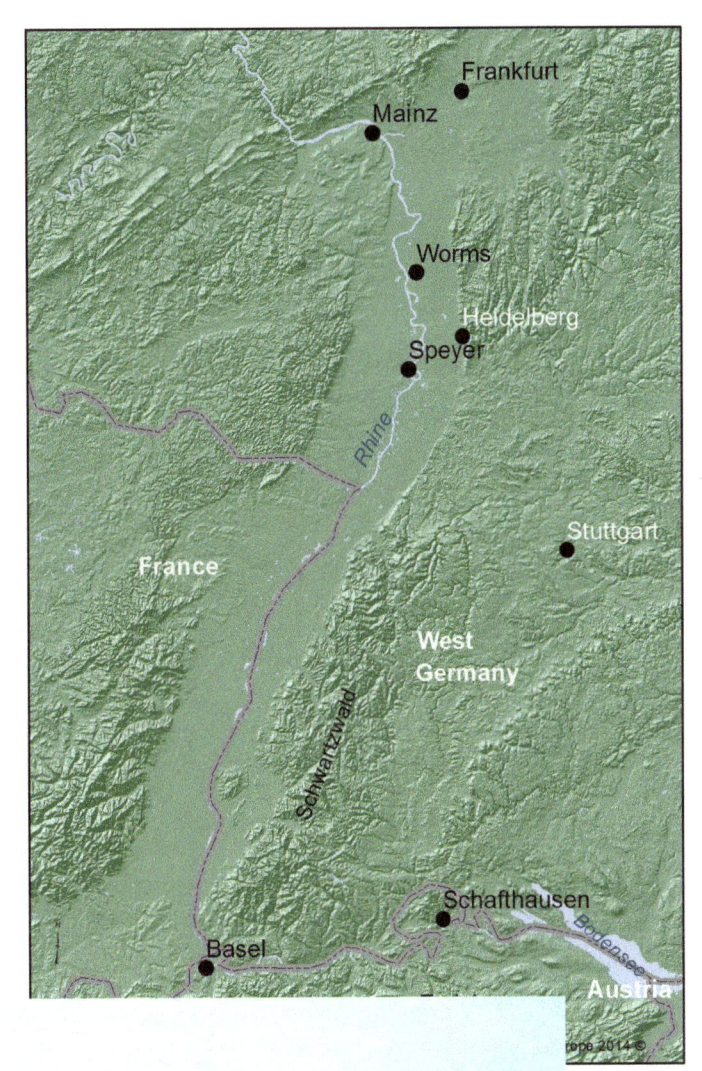

Alfred H. Siemens

I soon found a remarkable Schwarzwälder Hof, the typical rural farmstead of this mountain region; I contemplate it here again with pleasure, although the tree seems just a bit too deliberate. Friends joked that I must have carried an inflatable tree for my foregrounds.

The dwelling is to the right, stables, storage and workshops are to the left. The structure is massive, substantial, set into a slope, to allow easy access to an upper storage floor from the back. The peculiar overhanging roof provides deep shade in the summer's high sun, but access to winter's low sun too; the steepness sheds snow well. In materials and style it is rooted in regional or popular culture. The decorations are reserved and traditional, such a house looks venerable. On a later trip into the Schwarzwald I found that storage spaces beyond the living quarters in such houses are likely to be full of hand tools and field implements, evoking a regional history of agricultural technology as does a litter of discarded farm machinery anywhere else.

Christ hangs on many a roadside cross in southern Germany, inviting the passerby to reflection. One lunch break brought me some sober thoughts. I noticed I was close to the rim of a wartime fox hole and that the remains of trenches ran through the nearby trees.

Foxhole reflections

WWII had been over before I needed to be drafted. My knowledge of wars, pursued with some avidity as it happens, was out of books, magazines and museum displays. Because of the decisions of my Mennonite forebears to immigrate to Canada in the 1920s, I did not need to endure the subsequent deprivations that swept over Europe and the Soviet Union; I never had to be a fugitive. A member of a fortunate cohort in expansionist times in North America, I had a wide array of opportunities to work and study. I had this scholarship, this travel.

Although I was always affected deeply by what we in North America heard and read of hard times behind the Iron Curtain, the various flights and relocations, I was never in a position to investigate and write about the Mennonite 'Leidegang' as various of my good friends did, and very well too. My eventual focus on landscape studies and environmental history in the Latin American realm was a direction not taken by my Mennonite contemporaries. It was an odd thing, but that's where I happened to find my space for teaching, original research and the elaboration of intellectual integrity. Here in Europe I proceeded with what was before me: study of the liberal arts, working out my evangelical Christianity and geographical sensibilities, refinement of the Green Mackinaw and aesthetic enjoyment.

By the 9th of May, several weeks later than I had planned, I was coming down the Rheinebene, the Rhine River's plain. Asparagus was being harvested; women were digging gingerly into 18-inch ridges, extracting the shoots and smoothing over the holes. Signs advertised characteristic Rhine wines: *Liebfraumilch* for example. I laughed to myself, a wine named after a virgin and not just any virgin, but the Virgin Mary. And as for the milk – well.

I learned to head for the spires, that way I could get quickly to the heart of a strange town and through it, unless the church was prominent in my guidebook or something our teachers had told us came to mind.

'Stone book of history'

Here was the Romanesque cathedral of Speyer.[84] Binning had got the dictum I've put as a subhead from somewhere and it stuck with me; he impressed us deeply with what could be learned from monumental architecture. Romanesque is solid, heavy and massive, yet soaring, with that rounded arch; it alludes to Rome, of course, and pre-enlightenment Christianity.[85]

Such buildings have always seemed venerable to me, reserved but visually pleasing links with the past. The style was apparently the architectural innovation of its time, introduced in 1030 by Conrad II, Holy Roman Emperor, as an expression of imperial power. The style is mostly ecclesiastical, but it is sometimes echoed in vernacular architecture too, as I found it in the Apennines. I had already been shown such a church in London – 'Norman' or 'Medieval' are synonyms used in English – by my new gay friend and guide in the bowler hat, during our mad afternoon tour of London. I enjoyed the style again in Pisa's cathedral, its tower and its baptistery, course after course of delicate arches, not always accurately aligned. I've admired this style often in Spain, where it contends, more and more as one moves south through the Peninsula, with 'Moorish' elements coming up out of North Africa.

'Drink, drink, drink …'

How could one not stop in Heidelberg? It was already dark, the Schloss was spot lit, the town mirrored in the Neckar. Here was the German student world epitomized. It turned out to be a conflicted visit.

The Student Prince was the first feature film I ever saw, it's set in Heidelberg. I was already at UBC and it was passé no doubt by the time I saw it, but then how would I know. Going to movies wasn't the thing to do for an earnest, believing Mennonite boy. And then there's the drinking song. Irmy Klassen had assured me I would learn to appreciate alcohol when I got to Europe, and of course I did. A strong reservation remained about boozing and indeed is still there.

At the youth hostel, I found students sitting under trees; soon they were singing and dancing. I went up to my room and wrote dismissive thoughts into my diary. I have tried not to go beyond irony in my remarks about the keen, young Christian man, but this priggish judgement on the worldliness of others disgusts me now; I recall the various times during my years as an uncompromising believer when I was censorious, stand-offish, holier than thou.

Next day I got my photographic cliché, a bright colour transparency of the town from the terrace of the castle, complete with its inflatable tree. When I was through with it here at my computer it accorded better with my grimy recollections.

'Hier stehe ich, ich kann nicht anders'

The homestretch of my long spring trip to the Mediterranean still kept rewarding me with new sights and reflections. I came on Martin Luther at Worms, northwest of Heidelberg. There is this fine, well-known image of him by Lucas Cranach the Elder, as he appeared in 1533.[86] Worms was the place where princes of the Holy Roman Empire assembled in 1521; they judged Luther a menace to the Roman Catholic Church and the pope. He was to be put to death, but he escaped and would live another twenty-five years, go on to translate the New Testament from Greek to German and thus lay the basis for the High German language. I had already come on Luther: my mother gave me lessons in High German using the 'Luther' bible when I was a kid in Namaka, Alberta, where we had very few other books in the house. In high school and in Bible School, the bonding with this bible and with this German carried on.

Near the Worms cathedral, in a small museum, I found fascinating documents regarding the procedure of the 'Diet' regarding Luther and the papal bull against him. I was continuing to beaver away. At the Diet of Worms Luther uttered the famous statement I've set into the heading, 'Here I stand, I can do no other'. Historians are not so sure he actually said this, but the souvenir venders are unequivocal. Many years later I would find commemorative socks for sale in Luther's hometown, Wittenberg.

Alfred H. Siemens

Thumbing

By the time I had reached Mainz I had become really impatient; I put the moped on a train to Hamburg and thumbed the rest of the way. I had hitch-hiked long before going to Europe, it was an exuberant part of my 1940s and 50s. It belonged to breaking out, I suppose, although I had no oppressive home to get away from, quite the contrary, but I needed to explore, to test myself, to get beyond the horizon and feel other airs. This was intensified nicely by just that bit of risk. With Lawrence Warkentin I went off into the interior of British Columbia and tried sleeping rough in a city park. Such travel enlarged friendships, etched strong recollections. Every 'lift' brought an unpredictable exchange. There were gentlemen in fine cars; one of them explained that he didn't mind picking up clean-cut fellows, like ourselves, which helped our self-image. A raunchy honeymooning couple clowned for us. A truck driver asked me to roll a cigarette for him, a first for me and a lumpy cigarette for him. Then there was the drunk driver who invited Jim Poetker and myself into the back of his pickup. Came the curve he didn't make and the truck barrelled out among trees and rocks. Jim held on and was safe, I was catapulted over the cab, got resin on my pants in flight, and landed on a soft spot between rocks. With Harvey Dyck the concept of 'thumbing' was taken a bit further. We rode a freight train out of the Rockies from Jasper to Edmonton. Our travels, always a pleasure to recall, are to be written up in a separate context, if there is time. He would win the exchange scholarship to Hamburg the year after I did.

Out of Mainz I was picked up by a long-distance trucker; I soon learned some things about life on the Autobahn that I hadn't known before. He described the hijacking that could happen on long up-slopes, when you were crawling. Here was the bottle that he kept by his seat for when the fingers might appear over the edge of his window: whack, tumble and thump. He also explained the logistics of prostitution at the truck stops.

And then the encounter that had to happen sometime. On one of the last rides of the trip I became the guest of a homosexual, who made a complicated pass at me but backed off in the end, politely.

Re-entry

Now I needed to take up my studies again and also to face a new prospect that had opened for the coming year at UBC. Before leaving for the Mediterranean I had been invited to allow my name to stand for nomination to the presidency of VCF at UBC, 1955–56. The telegraphed invitation is on the next page. I replied as pencilled in on the right side, with one word – a bit of drama I found satisfying. I was 'willing.' I considered a second word but crossed it out, that must have sounded a bit too pious, I guess, even for me at the time. In the pile of mail that awaited me on return to Hamburg was a letter telling me that I had been elected. I found that sobering; I knew about the responsibilities, which in fact would turn out ot be quite demanding. Also my close personal identification with VCF and relationships with its animateurs would gradually became conflicted, but all that too is for another time.

Alfred H. Siemens

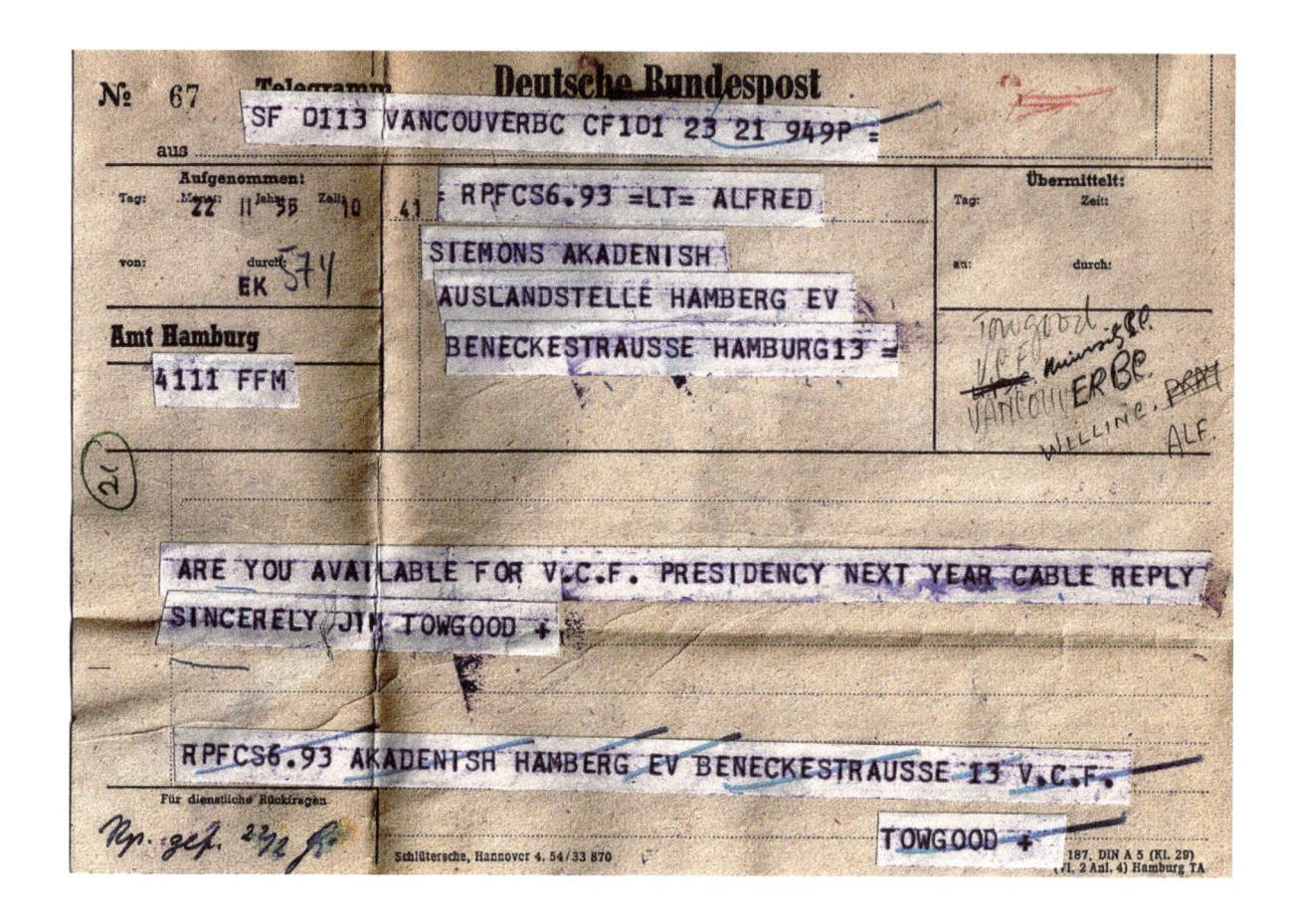

Two main benefits emerged from my last weeks at the university: Prof. Brünger's classes at the Geographical Institute and my reflections on the yields of the exchange. Brünger was the same professor who had counselled me in my first month. He was a big emphatic guy, fussed with his glasses and walked around the room. The subject was approximately Historical Geography, broadly conceived. He emphasized landscape and the passage of time, which was attractive to me. In one class he asked me if I knew about 'die Blaue Blume' – the blue flower. As it happened I did. A blue flower – of almost any variety – could be taken as a symbol of Romanticism, of love, longing, metaphysical longing, for the scarcely attainable, for distant horizons. As I've had to admit, such were and are my own inclinations. Thinking back now I must commend the intellectual scope and sensitivity of our professor.

On other days, we might well get deeply into the physical dynamics of landscape formation. I was suddenly surprised, I noted in my diary, that millions-of-years-figures no longer seemed ridiculous to me, as they did back in Bible School. Brünger also took the class on a fieldtrip to the town of Wedel, the same town to which I went most every weekend during my stay in Hamburg for evenings with my PAX friends. We stood together on the town square and heard about the Elbe River's hydrology, the susceptibility of the town to flooding – the sorts of basic physical environmental considerations that are useful in Human Geography. I liked that then and still do. Brünger also explained historic routes of movement through the region, cattle to market, for example, and the meaning of a Roland statue raised there in the sixteenth century.[87]

It alluded to the legend of a forceful figure fighting for independence on the side of cities against nobles, symbolizing market justice. His lower arm was a standard measure, disputes were settled under his gaze. Here was the meld of human and physical geography through time articulated in the open air to interested students that would become my own main stock in trade.

Geographers are scientists, Brünger maintained, they cannot surrender to an ultimate cause. They cannot recognize a creator who had simply set things up thus and so, who had willed them. If they do the wind goes out of their sails. They no longer need to investigate, to try to influence affairs consequentially.

I protested in my diary: "Of the denial of the first cause I [have] to be contemptuous ... All credit to logical thought. I desire more capacity for it. I do not consider it logical, wise or even just simply practical, however, to close the mind toward the supernatural ... my faith was not weakened".

Alfred H. Siemens

The virginal slide show

It was virginal in various senses; I inflicted it on the youth group at the Mennonite church in Hamburg one evening after my return to Hamburg from lemon blossom lands. It was about Italy, my developed images had just come back from Switzerland. I wonder now how I began my first interpretation of the 'south' to these people of the 'north'. That's one of the great things about working with slides, they can be shuffled, alternative arguments are easily possible. Did I begin with Venice? I probably did. Eventually I will have come to the Coliseum and the Roman Baths, and like that.

An opening tussle with the projector was just too prophetic; we had to fool about over a blown bulb. I would learn that an introductory protest by the projection or audio equipment is obligatory. It is a divine warning against arrogance. My Mexican friend Sergio Guevara has a better line on this: he feels it augurs well for the talk that follows, it flushes out the evil influences.

A girl from the youth group had come on to me strongly before my trip south and a stunningly awkward date had resulted, including an involvement with the girl's family. She was at my first slide show. She was still only sixteen years old but seemed to have matured during my absence. I confided to the diary that "Her unruly mop had become a beautifully modulated, evenly coloured auburn 'Italiano'. There were eyebrows and lipstick. She was very attractive, that was the trouble. My head was whirling and I was forgetting about her cool, sharp mind, her egotism, her calculated determination ... Several times our artfully sweeping glances crossed, fused, flickered and passed."

She had come to the slide show with her mother who was in a fur coat, and her impish little sister: they had me in their sights. I heard "*Ach wie schön*" [How nice!]. I would hear something like that again and again about my European slides. Within perhaps five years of my return to Canada the images and the reactions had become unbearable clichés for me. The slides went into metal boxes, where they remained unused for decades.

The mother asked specific questions to which she knew the answers; I was being examined and resented it. Apparently I did well, in the surreal sequel there was an urgent attempt to arrange another meeting, more slides, perhaps at their place, or at the youth retreat on the Pentecost weekend coming up. Would I be coming? Unfortunately not; I already had a study trip firmly planned. A touching *Abschied*, much flapping about, we really would need to meet again somewhere; I escaped.

SATURDAY, MAY 25: PENTECOST PUTTER

I'd been at the university only a few weeks and now I was off again. Coming on the trip in the diary it sounded frivolous, but on reflection I realized it had been quite in line with the purpose of my European experience. It was another facet of the same protracted exploration and it yielded well; it allowed me to see and appropriate an additional and most engaging body of art, more settlement morphology(!), more landscapes.

'Pfingsten' – Pentecost – is a long weekend for everyone just before the end of May. I made it into a trip that lasted from May 28–June 7 on a route that went down into the centre of Germany, West Germany then, and spooned around the rump of impenetrable East Germany.

"And when the day of Pentecost was fully come" the King James Bible says, "they were all with one accord in one place. And suddenly there came a sound from heaven as of a rushing mighty wind, and it filled all of the house where they were sitting. And there appeared unto them cloven tongues like as of fire, and it sat upon each of them. And they were all filled with the Holy Ghost." (Acts 2:1–4.) The mauve book of biblical drawings for children came to mind again when I retraced the putter.[88] I remember, as a kid, puzzling over the little flames above people's heads.

The moped was mulish most of the way. The carburetor had to come out at one point, the fuel line and the ignition remained problematical, all due to the mishandling by a freight handler on that first shipment from Hamburg to Munich. The lone spark plug had to be extracted for cleaning at intervals. The tires sprang repeated leaks by reason of pinched tubes or nails and required innumerable patches and manual pump-ups. One little evil-doer remained undetected in the tire and caused three flats in a row. I got agile at yanking even the back wheel out of its entanglements and slipping it back in.

Otherwise the riding was glorious. I had already enjoyed the smell of hay and appreciated dandelion fields in the Alpenvorland. Now it was fully summer, maturing grain and foliage gave the air a "bracing, strengthening scent". I napped in a meadow and got a sunburned face, sang hymns out over the sound of the motor.

"All Germany takes to the road [walking] on summer holidays … as we take drives back home." Lots and lots of ordinary people were out on *Spaziergänge*, some women in traditional dress, couples and young families, which made me envious, and walking clubs of various kinds. These are the *Wandervögel,* named after birds of passage, their insignia is the stork, which migrates between Africa and Europe.[89]

The clubs were founded early in the twentieth century, they were pre-eminently a German youth movement with ideals of back to nature, freedom, self-responsibility and adventure. Soon they had a nationalistic charge as well. They were outlawed by the Nazis, the Hitler Youth dominated the field, but they were re-established after WWII.[90] In the crowded youth hostels during the Pentecostal weekend, the Wandervögel were often boisterous, singing, sometimes just loutish; I couldn't get to sleep till they had gone at the crack of dawn.

Enlarging my store

I was able to keep my nerve, to set aside my concerns over conditions at home and add, item by item, to my store of geographical concepts and materials. Just outside of Hamburg I came on the diked orchard land on the floodplain of the Elbe River, known as 'das *Alte Land*'. This is a well maintained, functioning rural landscape eloquent of the long history of wetland settlement and land use in the low country of north central Europe. It's been prettied up for tourists, of course, well done too and completely absorbing.

One farmhouse front offered a bit of wisdom that I've recalled ruefully many times. Above the doorway a painter had lettered in: *En egen Hus, en egen Hof un Arbeit alle Dog: De meisten is dat Glück to grot, so säkt se sick en Plog.* / One's own house and land and steady work, that's too much good luck for most and so they look for trouble.

Alfred H. Siemens

The man and boy on the driver's seat of the oncoming wagon may well have grumbled or worse about the tourist who would talk of backwardness later when he showed his picture. I wish I could have let them know that it evokes the times I sat with my father on such a driver's seat in southern Alberta and learned to manage reins.

My putter southward, at something between twenty and thirty kilometres an hour, brought me again through the heathland, the Lüneburger Heide: anthropogenic, that is manmade through frequent use of fire and periods of cultivation. Much of it is closely settled now. Prehistoric stone structures, the *dolmen*, again indicated something of the mysterious early occupants of this land.

Farmsteads within and around the 'Heide' attracted me, as before: a traditional one, still with its prominent manure pile, and a more modern one, with the pre-eminent milk producer of the region, the Holstein cow, in pride of place. *Fachwerk*, the still common composite timber and brick construction, graced many towns to the south, as in Fritzlar. I was seeing it all with a larger conceptual toolkit than during the earlier excursions southwards with my Mennonite friends.

Marburg, a university town, aroused the young romantic's sensitivities to crocked streets and angled houses in an old town's core. It still happens to me whenever I get to wander in some part of Europe. After a certain time out on the western periphery of Canada the need arises to tread again on worn stone and read old inscriptions, maybe watch St. George kill a dragon.

Rounding the westward bulge of post WWII East Germany, I came on a series of old towns that have been grouped and vigorously sold to tourists as *Die Romantische Strasse*, The Romantic Road, including various towns, particularly Rothenburg, which is its key piece: settlement morphology commercialized.

Alfred H. Siemens

Green Mackinaw

Wood

In churches and museums along this 'Road' I came on wood carvings by Tilman Riemenschneider and Veit Stoss. They would give me some of the strongest aesthetic impressions of 1954–55. I already knew something of the pleasing feel, look and smell of wood split and carved. As a kid, I carved 1930s automobiles and then war planes out of whatever soft and straight grained wood I could get. A banking biplane hung from my ceiling, I did a twin fuselage Lockheed Lightning and a fairly good Mitchell bomber too: what a tail!

Some pages back I explained that Jim Draper, my brother-in-law Walter Bartsch and I acquired John Minarech's farm in the Columbia Valley. I came to appreciate the wooden artifacts of a pioneering lifetime all around us. I have one of John's split boards on the wall of my study; it faced the elements for a long time and still carries some dried lichen. There was also a time, after I had been to the new Museum of

Civilization near Ottawa, which opened in 1989, with its massive representation of west coast First Nations mastery of cedar that I began to scrounge drifted-in cedar logs from Spanish Banks and try my hand at splitting. I learned many things: honey-coloured freshly split cedar soon turns grey out in the open but that brings a new charm. Thump some cedar logs and they give a pleasing sound, promising a gong if one knows how to carve it out.

Back in German wood-carving country, a morning repair of the moped's rear tire had gone well and I was in a thankful mood as I entered Creglingen. "I enjoyed the harmony of the streets, the gossiping of women at doorways, the scamper of fowl and of children, and the very lovely chime of the church bell, a sweet smalltown-ish chime. People greeted each other as friends. There was a certain warmth everywhere, to which the enlivening, colouring sunlight added not a little." That was how Creglingen appeared to me that morning, indicating the effect of weather on one's attitude? No geographer has admitted to such bare-faced determinism for a long time. I like to think it was my inner buoyancy at that time and on that particular day. Under other circumstances and with a different predisposition the town might well have seemed dismal and parochial. There were signs every fifty feet, it seemed, pointing to the *Herrgottskirche* just out of town, which had an important altarpiece by Tilman Riemenschneider. Later I would also come on some fine carving by Veit Stoss in Bamberg.

No one will let you photograph these treasures yourself, of course, so I gathered imagery as I could find it on postcards and in a little publication called *Riemenschneider im Taubertal*, which carries no further bibliographical data. From these carefully photographed excerpts out of the artist's work I've chosen what particularly appealed to me, beginning with a self-portrait of the artist in a corner of a larger work. His deftly moulded hat is textured with the grain of the wood from which it came. I like the apostles Peter and Andrew, the one solicitous of the other and two details of expressive hands, one just lifting a robe, others agitated in some intense discussion, presumably theological. Termites, which must have been the perpetual plague of this art, have left their holes here and there. I found a ravaged Christ, as though he had just been with Schweitzer in Africa. In another corner a guard slept at a grave.

Veit Stoss, I came on some of his work in Bamberg: the holy family fleeing to Egypt.

Green Mackinaw

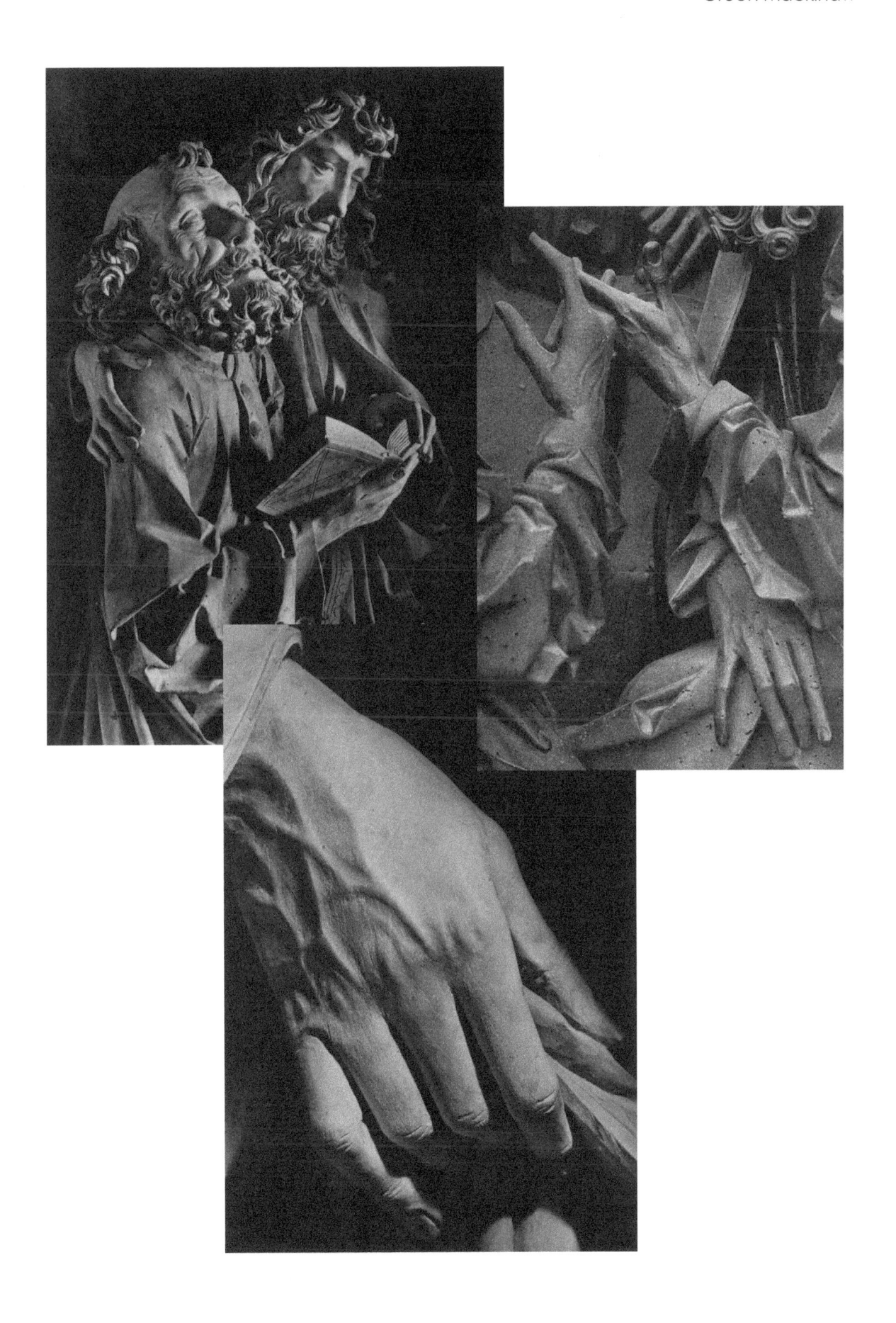

190

Alfred H. Siemens

191

Green Mackinaw

Alfred H. Siemens

Sunday, the 5th of June, at about 6:00 p.m. I found myself in a little place called Uelzen, 110 km from Hamburg. I decided I would really sprint back now. At 11:00 p.m. I was at the door of Papenkamp 16. I had made it in five hours, which works out to an average speed of about twenty-two kilometres per hour! In my mail was a letter from home requesting I return as soon as possible.

"I must and I will go to assist." I wasn't really deprived of much; I'd filled the time I had had quite well and surely there would be other trips to Europe in the future. I suspect they regarded my puttering about the German countryside as more than a little frivolous. They were ill, depressed, felt threatened and worried about their future; they obviously required help. Mary had done very well but now needed spelling off. OK. I was to arrange a flight home within a few weeks, they would find the money.

WEDNESDAY, JUNE 8: CONCLUDING EARLY

It was summer along the Alster, the tributary that comes from the north into the Elbe River and enlarges into a lovely lake in the heart of Hamburg. I've shown it in winter, with branches bare all around, and at night when it becomes a reflecting pool. The war's damage to the trees, quite dramatic in the early imagery, is just detectable among the summer foliage on the left. I wasn't enjoying summer days so much now as reviewing visually the city I had come to appreciate, and making other last moves.

Some of the remaining time was spent at the little table in front of my window in Papenkamp 16 laboriously mounting slides between thin glass covers; I meant the slides to last me a good long while and the covers did serve their purpose until they had to be removed in preparation for scanning all these many years later. I was beginning to assemble my teaching resources: art, landscapes, monuments and especially examples of buildings not shaped by architects but by traditional wisdom.[91] Catherine Griffiths, who helps me in all matters graphic, assembled a mosaic of diagnostic dwellings referred to in these pages, much like I would later regularly lay out slides on a light table in preparation for a lecture.

Alfred H. Siemens

I didn't get much traction with the analysis of dwellings when I proposed it for doctoral research in Geography at the University of Wisconsin, as I've said. It wasn't 'problematical' enough. And it was a youthful enthusiasm that came up against the hard-nosed requirements of one of the leading geography graduate programs in North America. I sought out alternatives, became hard-nosed myself. In the discipline the interpretation of vernacular architecture, particularly symbolization in the built environment, eventually became quite sexy, but by then I was deeply into other things.

Sensitivity to the installations, the material things that encompass daily life persisted during the many years of my field investigations in Latin America. I emphasized the pragmatic as I pursued questions related to landscapes, remains of ancient agriculture and settlements in tropical lowland landscapes, and then the broader subject of environmental history. Sometime in the 1960s I came on this dwelling along the Candelaria River, in the state of Campeche, Mexico. The photograph itself could now be considered a museum piece: a solitary settler's homestead along a river, surounded by the material elements of traditional peasant adaptation to forested humid tropics. Such places are mostly modernized now: galvanized metal and cement blocks have become the building materials, a solar panel provides power for a few appliances, particularly something that plays music, and it's likely that a pickup truck is parked next to the house. The older transportational function of the river has been taken over by a web of roads.

Poetic interstices often compensated me for the tedium of sytematic observation in aid of the stricter 'scientific' considerations in which I was involved, as here on the outskirts of the town of Candelaria along that same river – a counterweight or perhaps just a continuation by other means.

During my last weeks in Hamburg I went for a walk around the docks: grey sky, sea-scented breeze. It occurred to me that during my time away I had not felt loneliness so much as adjusted to solitude, in fact I was seeking it out. It allowed untrammeled observation and focus, it was one of the year's gains. I would have to adjust if one day I wanted to live with someone, and I did want that.

The entertainments of the last weeks make up quite an agreeable list – evenings well spent. *Gershwin Night at the Musikhalle*, "properly sawed and blown by the *Hamburg Kammerorchester.*" It didn't seem jazzy enough, even to me at the time. I would come to appreciate Gershwin's *Rhapsody in Blue* very much when I got to lecture about New York years later. An open air Opera Festival was on at the botanical gardens, called *Planten & Blomen*. An old Mennonite Brethren interdiction against opera cast its shadow over the performance. I pronounced the music as "really quite harmless". I went to see *Das Kleine Teehaus*, a staged version of what would become the movie, *Teahouse of the August Moon;* I perceived it as an appropriate "satire on American attempts to establish democracy on Okinawa." One more night at the movies: a newsreel on Le Mans racing, a documentary on Canada, which made me homesick, a good Disney cartoon, then Hitchcock's classic *Rear Window*.[92]

A student parliament was also in there somewhere, "A typical student-type tangle of procedure, but for all that probably very indicative of the nature of even the good real parliaments." My eventually quite well-developed disgust with politics was beginning.

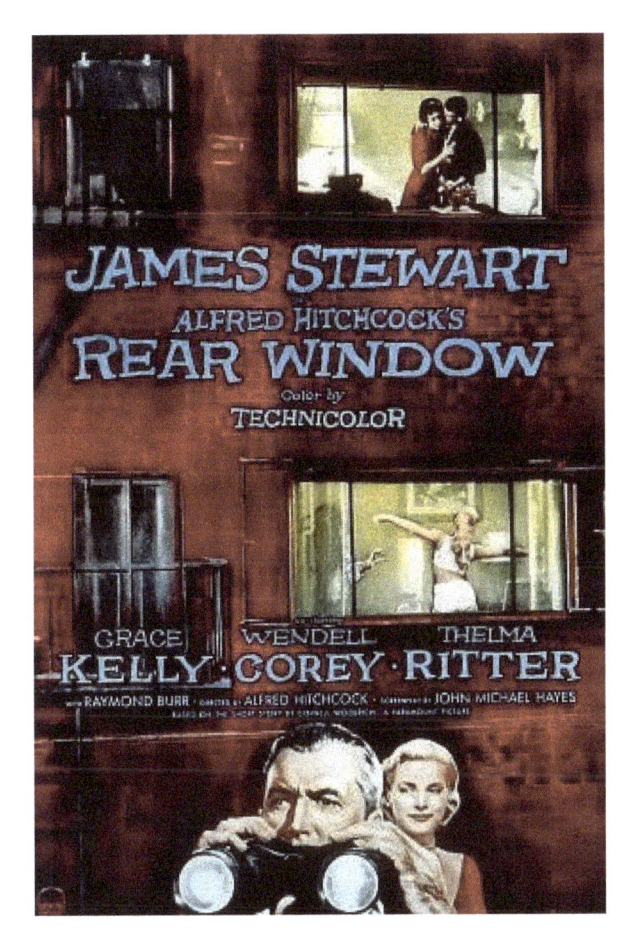

I was still attending some seminars and lectures at the university too, so here comes one by Arnold Toynbee, no less, on *Religion in History and Culture*. I felt endorsed, a distinguished academic and a believer was referring to God and Christ and the course of history in ways with which I could heartily concur. I rather expected already that I would become an academic, but I intended to be a believing academic.

Before I left for the Mediterranean Bob Detweiler had shown me the Reeperbahn, the nightclub district with its side streets of whores in the windows. Now Leonard Gross, one of the PAX group, asked me to show it to him. My sanctimonious observations in the diary are quite funny.

There's also a long entry in the diary on a faculty member in Education, Prof. Dr. Froese – such double-barrelled honorifics were common at the university – but my memory fails me here. I can't remember how I met him or even how he looked. He was kind enough to invite me into to his home. Once again I was able to observe an attractive marriage and home life. Politeness prevailed, the atmosphere was intellectually vibrant, the humour sharp. Love had obviously persisted after seven years of marriage, which looked to me then as a long time. The parent's authority seemed to be rooted in respect. The children were being carefully reared, they were not afraid but not undisciplined either. If I had come on another day I might well have gained other impressions in this home, but no matter, I wanted something like this. And my libido was a barely banked fire.

The question of reunification was very near the surface in German minds for decades after the war and was certainly in the media during 1954–55. Froese had studied education in the 'Ost Zone' – East Germany. He felt it would not be good psychology or good political tactics to assume an attitude of superiority in ideological matters. There was need for caution and tolerance in the encounters between the two worlds. The Berlin Wall did finally come down in 1989 and reunification could

Alfred H. Siemens

begin, but the disparate conditioning of more than forty years of separation between 'Wessis,' those of the former 'West Zone,' and 'Ossis,' those of the former 'East Zone,' has remained difficult to bridge. I have tested for this during all of my subsequent visits to Germany.

Froese invited me to his seminar on *Glaube und Erziehung (Faith and Education)*; it was an important lesson for me regarding a way of teaching. Participants presented papers, relaxed discussion ensued, only indirectly guided with no apparent concern about the completion of any particular portion of material. I liked this and determined to advocate it on return, but it wouldn't be until I was well into my graduate work before seminars would be my regular fare. After retirement from UBC I mostly taught that way in the various short intensive courses I gave at Mexican universities. And every Wednesday for many years a small group of us, all past our 'best before' dates, met at the house of Phil Wagner, geographer emeritus at Simon Fraser University, for an amiable seminar, vaguely patterned after seminars in geography given at the University of California in Berkley during the remarkable time of Carl O. Sauer. The agendas were usually unpredictable, the discussions often deeply moving. One day early in 2014 he left us.

Evaluation

What had been learned during my year abroad would not yield me any credits toward my degree, in fact no one at the University of Hamburg nor at UBC would take much notice of what I had or had not studied, there would be no report to write. Rounding off was a personal necessity, then as now.

It had taken me a while in fall of 1954 to appreciate the absence of prerequisites: there were no formal sequences in courses, first this, then that and finally that. There were implicit sequences, of course, but it took a good deal of discussion, thought and time to work those out. The immediate and agreeable challenge was to sort out my own inclinations and to find out what was logical under the circumstances, mostly just what was interesting. I was quite unprepared for some of the seminars I wandered into and made some memorable faux pas but I was able to swallow them and continue.

I had set myself the objective of finishing one methodological paper during my time in Hamburg, but I didn't finish it. I still needed deadlines, all-nighters, and felt a bit guilty about this. On the other hand, I had observed widely, grazed intellectually, beavered conscientiously – various metaphors can be applied – I had certainly appropriated the freedom to roam. Such a year abroad really did constitute LIBERAL ARTS; its realizations would stay with me.

An evaluation of the exchange *per se* happened in amiable discussions with Wolfram Kretchmar who had been on exchange from Hamburg to UBC a year or two before and Peter Jacob who was due to come to UBC in 1955–56. Wolfram had already written me a long and nutritious letter while I was still in Vancouver, filling me in about what I might expect in Hamburg. He now entertained us with his impressions of students at UBC, about rowdy, noisy life in 'Acadia Camp,' a converted WWII army barracks that served as one of the main student residences. He had been amused at the informal clothes and the curious dating practises. He cautioned Peter about the forced march our academic system required through rigidly defined sequences of courses and about the fevered cramming for exams. That reinforced what I had already come to think as well.

Peter helped me interpret the German students that had surrounded me in Hamburg. They were moderately liberal, as was the populace, he maintained. Nationalism such as had prevailed before the war, was not desired, such socialism as there was among the students was superficial. The general security and quality of life in the country had improved markedly by the mid 1950s, the class struggle and push for economic betterment were no longer so urgent. I wasn't so sure about that; I was meeting penurious students who fantasized about the rich life in Canada.

Aside from my personal, Christian imperatives, I could not have pointed to any great urgencies amongst us either. We were not much different from the German students he had described. We were 'seizing the day,' preparing ourselves for prosperity, proud to be Canadian, by and large, not animated by anything very revolutionary. True, we were apprehensive of how the Cold War might yet heat up and quite fearful of possible atomic warfare, but confident of our country's positive role in the world and of its security.

I did meet the previous Canadian scholarship holder but I didn't note his name, and he seemed to have spent little time in study, hadn't taken the whole thing very seriously; I couldn't credit him.

Alfred H. Siemens

Last look around

'Der Michel', the tower of St. Michael's Lutheran Church, is on innumerable souvenirs. It is protestant baroque in style and widely taken as a symbol of the city. A statue of St. Michael vanquishes the devil over its main entrance. The church was built and rebuilt from the mid-seventeenth century onward. Ships coming in along the Elbe still take it as a landmark. I found it particularly handsome and took note of it often from various angles during my stays in the city, particularly now that I was about to leave.

In two successive visits to the Museum for Hamburg History,[93] I deliberately reviewed the table models of the city's history, a working model of one of its railway stations, costumes, ships and prehistoric finds. I've often thought since that museology would have been a fine alternative career.

Peter took me to the stock exchange; I was fascinated by the business elite doing their Hamburgian thing. We also toured the harbour, heard the clank of the cranes. We rode the little steamer on the Alster – it appears some pages earlier – we sat at a sidewalk café, and eventually ate at the Rathaus.

Peter stressed the city's Hanseatic, republican background, which already had been impressed upon me, it's the first thing you read about this city. The emphases, Peter maintained, were always on a maximum of independence, on commercial rather than militaristic or courtly functions. Manners were refined, but people spoke directly. Titular propriety was played down. There were senators who declined decoration, dignitaries who preferred to remain incognito. Modesty was the proper thing, it was strutted as others might strut ceremony. All this was probably more about Peter and his circle than about the townspeople in general and did not negate what I had learned already about life on the street. Everyone remembered the war, of course, but it was already distant and unreal. They were as engulfed in materialism as anyone in the West.

Alfred H. Siemens

Helmut Funke had already made the same point in an incisive talk to the youth group the previous fall. We were to maintain spiritual values; post-war and post-recovery materialism had become alarming among Mennonites.

I had already photographed the harbour, composed the forms and lines as I usually do, and listened to the clanking of loading. Later, I found a more muscular view, painted not long before I had come on the scene.[94] Hamburg was known once again for shipbuilding.

A British aircraft carrier happened to be in, here was an echo of WWII. Hamburg had been in the British zone of occupation since the war, but this was officially over by May of 1955. The aircraft carrier was probably not long for this harbour.

Jungfernstieg means 'maiden's walk'. Evidently families used to take their unmarried daughters for walks here on Sunday afternoons hoping to attract husbands. Consider the map on the opposite page, lively and eloquent, a worthy fetish.[95] Begin with my own focal point: *Dammtor* the S-Bahn terminal, named after, I speculate: a gate in the old city wall, a gate that led on to the great early dyke that created the lovely inner-city lake, the Binnen Alster. I remember that in the cache of the materials brought back I have a history of the city and in a short while I have all that confirmed and I have barely resisted becoming entangled here. The Binnen Alster was originally a millpond, the circum-city fortifications were put in place in the seventeenth century, flattened in 1820, wonderful things like that.[96]

The university is up to the north, my frequent trudges southeastward took me past a striking monument on the *Stephansplatz* and down to the inexpensive eating places near the Jungfernstieg, occasionally further south to the Rathaus, which is marked in red. This was my daily ambit; on weekends I went to the Mennonite church west of the old city wall, in what was once a suburb: Hamburg-Altona, and usually much further west as well to Wedel, where the PAX boys lived. Roughly between the two was my room at Papenkamp 16, with the window on the garden and what must be an allusion in its name, now that I think of it, to old monastery lands.

Green Mackinaw

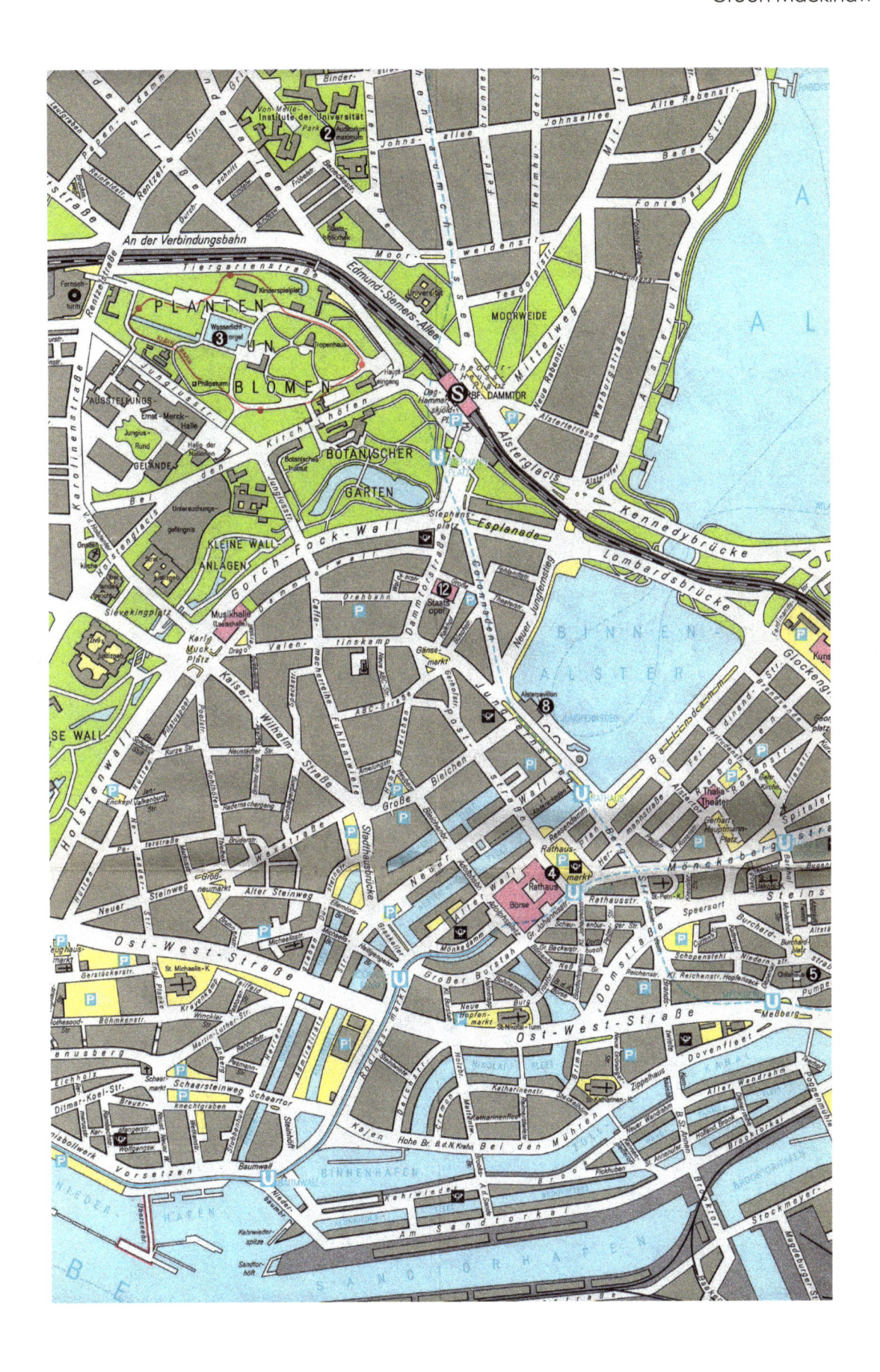

Alfred H. Siemens

The monument on Stephansplatz was one of the few Nazi memorials remaining in the country. It was built in 1936 to honour the members of the Hanseatic Infantry who died in the Franco-Prussian War and also those who died in WWI.[97] The soldiers are anonymous duplicates of one another. Battle is glorified and the inscription reads: "Germany must live, even if we must die." In 1955 nothing had yet been put up in this city for the dead of WWII.

It's June; I'm on one of my last walks downtown along the Jungfernstieg. Some people are sitting at open air tables on the left, but there must have been a bit of a chill because people are wearing light coats, the car in the foreground is an Opel, produced in Germany by a subsidiary of General Motors, and in front of it is a Mercedes. Occasionally I would see a large American car – far out of scale. The Germans had a word for them: 'Strassenkreutzer', that is 'cruisers of the street', and I think they meant warships.

Among the 1954 collection of Hamburg watercolours that I have resorted to repeatedly there is a view of an industrial area south of the Elbe River.[98] Quite another Hamburg: smokestacks here, not spires. My impressions of the city and my renditions had been quite selective.

Suddenly Denmark

Before finding out that I would need to go home early I had planned a trip to Copenhagen; a Danish friend at UBC had planted that idea, but I had dismissed it now as too rushed – and expensive. I supposed I would be coming back to Europe eventually anyway. Unsuspecting, I went along to what must have been my penultimate Sunday visit to my PAX friends in Wedel. The parents of one of them, Bob Steiner, were there and invited me to come with the three of them in their car to Copenhagen, expenses paid, company for Bob and help in navigation, leaving immediately. Why not?

Alfred H. Siemens

Crossing lowlands in north central Europe allowed me to enlarge on what I had already seen in travel to spiritual retreats with my Mennonite friends during the previous fall. Holsteins, the black and whites milk producers were to be seen in the fields again. Cold winds blew in here off the North Sea in winter, sensible to hunker down in the landscape, to accommodate people and animals, to provide storage as well, all in one extended building with few doors or windows.

This windmill attracted me on the brief trip north in 1955; on later travels on the continent and in England I became aware of an old system of signalling with the blades of a windmill. This one, if I'm not mistaken, is signalling that a service is needed, a stone mason to 'sharpen' a grinding stone or a carpenter to repair a wooden member. Diking around the mill indicates it is probably a pumper, keeping the water level down in the surrounding lowland. Who knows? But it's satisfying to generate hypotheses as one moves through a landscape, questions one would ask local people if one had the chance.

Once into Denmark I managed to halt our fast trip to Copenhagen enough for these 'grab shots' of rurality: beautiful red animals on green, which I find now are probably of the 'Danish Red' breed, excellent milkers too, widespread in Eastern Europe. And then a farmhouse, I had been avid for farmhouses all that year. I've taken Jim Houston's *A Social Geography of Europe* from its shelf.[99] In Oxford, he had introduced me to aerial photography of ancient agriculture, lent me his bicycle and fed me oatmeal. The book was published in 1953 but I didn't appreciate it until some years after my return. There on page 127 he identifies the "Danish Farm house." The book is rich with examples of the morphology of dwellings and settlement, it is sensitive to relationships between human constructions and the physical environment, it probes the origins of rural and urban forms and sets it all into the human geographical theory of the time. This was my kind of material.

The Steiners were lovely people, we got along well and they paid for everything. Bob and I manoeuvred smoothly through town and country, the parents were amazed. We 'did' Copenhagen: Tivoli, fish wives at the harbour, the famous mermaid on a rock, the changing of the guard at the royal palace, the house of Hans Christian Anderson, the whole Danish bit, and soon I realized I was involved in the superficial clichéd tourism that I had inveighed against earlier. Moreover, I was now likely to be seen by locals as a well-off American, better off than most Europeans of the time, as one of those who were running about Europe as children in a wonderland. The cordial travel with these kind people thus had its dark side for me which, of course, I could not discuss with them. It became one of the main lessons of 1954–55: avoid thoughtless travel.

Wouldn't I now please just come with them on the rest of their remaining itinerary in Europe, all expenses paid? I swallowed hard but sorry, I really did have to go home. Would I at least come with them to Berlin during the brief time that I had left? That was attractive and would have provided an excellent baseline for later visits, when the wall had gone up and come down. But there was some permit that I wouldn't be able to get in time, so I had to demur.

Full circle

In the correspondence I saved there is this note from Doris Nikkel, my good friend Helmut Funke's fiancée, who did secretarial work for the Mennonite Church at Hamburg-Altona including its youth group. It's charmingly intricate and impossible to translate directly. She says she's been asked to ask me to do a final biblical meditation at the 'Jugendstunde,' the meeting of the youth group. Oh and I would be very welcome to attend the business meeting beforehand too. They had liked my virginal slide show some weeks before and I think she was now asking for more pictures. In any case they wanted to enjoy a bit more of my presence. Twice she uses the word, 'herzlich;' the invitation is meant to be affectionate. I cannot imagine a more gratifying conclusion for 1954–55. It began with acceptance into this group and ended with their appreciation. I had already known such affirmation, solidarity and support from my VCF friends at UBC and would feel it again later on in more secular terms from my students, especially from my Mexican graduate students.

> 13.6.55
>
> Lieber Alfred!
>
> Ich soll Dich hiermit darum bitten, am Donnerstag die Bibelarbeit zu machen! Vielen Dank! Davor ist Komitee. Dazu bist Du natürlich auch herzlich eingeladen. Es wäre sogar schön, wenn Du kämst schon wegen der Bilder. Und wir wollen doch Deine Anwesenheit auch noch etwas geniessen!
>
> Also auf Wiedersehen demnächst!
> Herzliche Grüsse
> Doris

Three Mennonite friends, emerge most particularly from the recollections of 1954–55. They shared my spiritual commitment, each had an easy sense of humour and cared for others: Helmut Funke, a German, leader of the youth group at the Hamburg Altona Mennonite Church; Nettie Redekop, a Canadian, 'housemother' of the PAX contingent at Wedel, just outside of Hamburg; Bob Detweiler, an American, leader of that same PAX contingent.

They came out of various Mennonite subgroups. I doubt that I could specify their exact affiliations or that I have their actual positions right here now, but maybe it doesn't matter; in my diary and in my memory they are my very sympathetic cohort. We had countless warm exchanges on things spiritual and otherwise at meals, over the washing up, on the road to a retreat, at entertainments and of course in devotional meetings. Within a year, for various reasons, all three of them had left Hamburg.

On the evening of July 2, the day before my departure, I went to visit the PAX people. They gave me their farewells and of course I was deeply moved. Walking to the Wedel S-Bahn station, stars overhead, the diary says, I "received" Psalm 91:10–12. Such 'receiving' is not so different from the realization of any other creative idea: conditioning, ready data, receptivity, a particular moment and who knows what else, converge to produce it fully formed. One hopes one remembers it until there is a chance to write it down or talk about it. The exalted language of the Bible provides excellent articulation. In any case on that night it felt like a benediction:

> "There shall no evil befall thee,
> Neither shall any plague come nigh unto thy dwelling.
> For He shall give his angels charge over thee,
> To keep thee in all thy ways.
> They shall bear thee up in their hands …" (Psalms 91:10–13)

SUNDAY, JULY 3: LIFT OFF

It was a beautiful summer day, I said farewell to the Gross family, the owners of Papenkamp 16, looked back up to the window of my room, boarded the S-Bahn for the last time at Kleinflottbeck station, changed at Dammtor, remembering the 'Würstchen und heisse Milch' at its snack bar on cold winter mornings, and went on to the airport. Several friends from the youth group were there to see me off.

This would be no direct flight, there were no such flights across the Atlantic, one flew around its margins on propeller planes with limited ranges. I was leaving on a DC4 of Icelandic Airlines, *Luftleidir*, which pioneered low cost Atlantic crossings to Europe. In the 1960s it would become known as the 'hippie' airline.[100]

My itinerary to Vancouver took twenty-two flying hours, we came down in Luxemberg, Reyklavik, Goose Bay, Labrador, and then New York, where I overnighted and did some wandering about. My fascination with the city, with *The New Yorker* magazine, *The New York Times* and Gerschwin's *Rhapsody in Blue* would come later. We touched down in Toronto and then went on over the Prairies to Vancouver.

Alfred H. Siemens

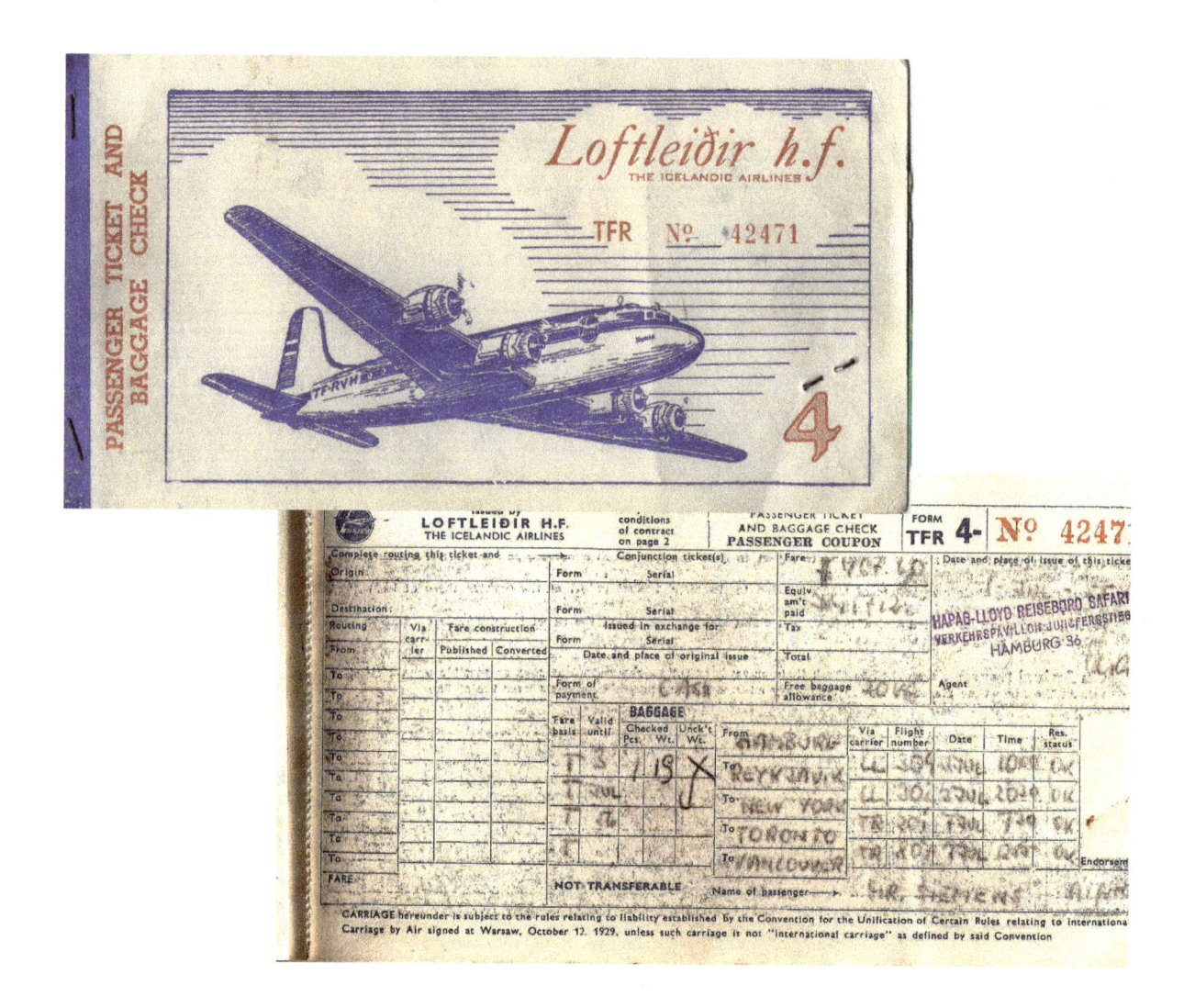

Cumbersome, all this, but it was in fact a a fine introduction to flying. I was thrilled. The voyage out had been nostalgic, the old way to cross the Atlantic, the flight back had the lustre of newness. There would be hundreds of commercial flights in my future, and then from the early 1960s onward dozens of flights in small chartered planes as I developed my discipline of aerial landscape photography, but I never lost my appreciation for flying.

This first bright day in the air was smooth, later we did have to do some white knuckle slaloms between storm clouds over the Prairies.

It would be apparent to me very soon that the aerial view was a privileged view, I have continued to feel this way even though flying has become drudgery and most passengers around me care little; they pull down the shades. For me there remains much to be found out and appreciated from this vantage point.

Once we were airborne from Hamburg, the landscape seemed to move, not the plane; it has always felt this way to me and I've wanted to grasp what's there before it flees. "Very quickly Hamburg spread out beneath us and began to move away. There was a haze over the 'City' but the Alster, the spires, some bridges and streets came through recognizably. For just a few minutes the magnificent harbour and the Elbe were in sight, then all was gone."

I suppose I will have seemed quite calm to seatmates, but I felt an agitation of emotions: the thrill of flight, the warm anticipation of reunion with my parents and Mary. But might not there be a lingering resentment? I had been on a lark, educational maybe, but a lark nevertheless, while they had had a tough time. I would need to step carefully and make myself useful. I already missed the friends and the good times of Hamburg. My love life! I would need to make some moves. There was the rude prospect of going back to work on the railway for the remainder of the summer, behind that a demanding winter at UBC with the responsibility for the VCF chapter and the concluding studies for my B.A. "Rather sticky thoughts", as the diary says.

Fortunately I had a book, I always have a book, sufficiently captivating to dim such thoughts, in this case Ivan Turgenev's *Fathers and Sons*, in a German edition.[101] I read the whole thing between Hamburg and Vancouver. I found it here yesterday, on a back shelf: great German, yellowed paper. It fell open to page 113 where I had strongly marked a passage, which points out the usefulness of finding some way of loosening taut strings, of dissipating self- absorbed thoughts, of slowing down. I guess I needed that during the flight, and still do, again and again.

I have usually preferred a window seat, even at night, I tend to peer into the darkness for spatters of light that signal, say, that we have crossed water and are coming over a coast, which I then like to match in my mind with remembered maps. I love to watch sunrise or sunset tint the wings, especially when day and night are ambiguous as one flies westward through time zones, racing the sun, or going over the pole. I don't care much for turbulence, of course, but quite like to bore into and out of clouds.

Somewhere over the Atlantic we were served dinner and then to finish – this is not in my diary but firmly in my memory – a blonde flight attendant passed me a coffee and cognac; it seemed immensely civilized.

ACKNOWLEDGEMENTS

Alice read all the early drafts and many of the revised passages too; she managed to remain wonderfully supportive.

Catherine Griffiths has helped me in matters graphic and computational for many years. This project would not have been possible without her.

Valuable comments came from the following readers of a penultimate version – in alphabetical order: Yvonne Brown, Anne and Harvey Dyck, Mary Anne and Harold Epp, Erna Friesen, Jake Friesen, Maija Heimo, Peter Rahn, Helen and John Ratzlaff, Frankie Robinson, Barbara Siemens, Fred Schwartzmann, Mary Taylor, and Victor Vogt.

Editors at Friesen Press in Victoria were very helpful. Astra Crompton amiably shepherded a rather willful manuscript through the preparation process.

I am grateful for permission to reproduce several photographs: to Rob Stuart of Austin Works for an Austin A40, to Dirk Detweiler for the picture of his father Bob Detweiler and to the Jewish Historical Society of British Columbia for the portrait of Dr. B.C.Binning who was photographed by Fred S. Schiffer [October 8, 1966]. Jewish Museum and Archives of BC, L.24847.

ENDNOTE

[1] Wikipedia contributors. "Mackinaw cloth." *Wikipedia, The Free Encyclopedia.* Wikipedia, the Free Encyclopedia, 13 May. 2016. Web. 1 Sep. 2016.

[2] Espenshade Jr.,Edward B., Editor. *Goodes World Atlas Thirteenth Edition.* Chicago: Rand McNally and Company. 1970 Print.

[3] Siemens, Alfred H. *Between the Summit and the Sea: Central Veracruz in the Nineteenth Century.* Vancouver: University of British Columbia Press. 1990. Print.

[4] Siemens, Alfred H. *Tracings.* In process.

[5] Sacks, Oliver. "Speak, Memory." *The New York Review of Books*, NYRev Inc., 21 Feb. 2013, http://www.nybooks.com/articles/2013/02/21/speak-memory/.

[6] Cowles, Gregory. "'The Art of Memoir,' by Mary Karr." *The New York Times*, The New York Times, 24 Oct. 2015, http://www.nytimes.com/2015/10/25/books/review/the-art-of-memoir-by-mary-karr.html.

[7] Mallen, Leah. "Get Inside The Binning House." *Coast Modern*, Twofold Films, 2 May 2013, http://coastmodernfilm.com/2009/06/24/get-inside-the-binning-house-july-1-2009/. **Need to get permission from Publisher AHS working on it**

[8] Canadian Pacific Railroad, "CPR Dining Car" http://www8.cpr.ca/cms/English/General+Public/Heritage/Photo+Gallery/Rolling+Stock/default.htm Accessed April 2012.

[9] Siemens, Alfred H. *The Americas: a Comparative Introduction to Geography.* Scituate, MA : Duxbury Press, 1977.

[10] Dion, Huguette. "Le Château Frontenac." File:Château Frontenac, Ville De Québec.JPG, Wikimedia Commons, 26 July 2012, https://commons.wikimedia.org/wiki/file:ch%c3%a2teau_frontenac,_ville_de_qu%c3%a9bec.jpg. Accessed May 29, 2016

[11] Espenshade, Edward B Jr. ed. *Goode's World Atlas.* 13th ed., Chicago: Rand McNally, 1970. p. 134.

[12] Ackroyd, Peter. *London: the Biography.* Reprint, London: Knopf Doubleday Publishing Group, 2003. *Reprint.*

[13] Geni. "*Interior of Pitt River Museum.*" Wikimedia Commons, 22 Sept. 2015, https://commons.wikimedia.org/wiki/file:interior_of_pitt_rivers_museum_2015.jpg. Accessed May 29, 2016

[14] Frere, Sheppard, and St Joseph J. K. S., *Roman Britain from the Air.* Cambridge: Cambridge University Press, 1983. p. 208.

[15] Siemens, Alfred H. "Searching Out Prehispanic Landscapes in Mesoamerica by Means of Aerial Reconnaissance." *The Oxford Handbook of Mesoamerican Archaeology*, 2012, pp. 552–566. doi:10.1093/oxfordhb/9780195390933.013.0039.

[16] Heimo, Maija. *Prehispanic Wetland Agriculture South of Laguna Mandinga, Veracruz, Mexico. Testing Postulations of Water Management and Agricultural Intensification*. Vancouver: University of British Columbia, 1998. Unpublished M.A.Thesis.

[17] United Kingdom Government. "Spitfire Camera Gun Still." *File:Spitfires Camera Gun Film Shows Tracer Ammunition.jpg*, Wikipedia, 14 Nov. 2011. https://en.wikipedia.org/wiki/file%3aspitfires_camera_gun_film_shows_tracer_ammunition.jpg. This artistic work created by the United Kingdom Government is in the public domain.

[18] UBC Alma Mater Society. *The Totem 1954*, Vancouver: University of British Columbia. 1954. p. 152.

[19] Iliff, David. "A Panoramic View of the Oxford Skyline." *File:Oxford Skyline Panorama from St Mary's Church - Oct 2006.Jpg*, Wikipedia, 15 Oct. 2006, https://en.wikipedia.org/wiki/file:oxford_skyline_panorama_from_st_mary%27s_church_-_oct_2006.jpg.

[20] Baker, John. "A40 Dorset &Amp; Devon." John Baker's Austin Memories, John Baker, http://www.austinmemories.com/styled-33/styled-36/index.html. August 2016, Image is used with permission of author.

[21] Hoskins, W. G. *The Making of the English Landscape*. London: Penguin. 1955.

[22] seier+seier. "Wells Cathedral, Wells, Somerset." *File:Wells Cathedral, Wells, Somerset.jpg*, Wikimedia Commons, 25 July 2010, https://commons.wikimedia.org/wiki/file:wells_cathedral,_wells,_somerset.jpg.

[23] Pingstone, Adrian. "The Inverted Arch in Wells Cathedral." *File:Wells.cathedral.inverted.arch.arp.jpg*, Wikipedia, 29 Nov. 2006, https://en.wikipedia.org/wiki/file%3awells.cathedral.inverted.arch.arp.jpg. Accessed May 29, 2016. Photographed by Adrian Pingstone and placed in the public domain.

[24] Evans, Federick. "A Sea of Steps." Wikimedia Commons, 1 May 2014, https://commons.wikimedia.org/wiki/file:a_sea_of_steps_--_wells_cathedral_lacma_m.2008.40.736(1_of_3).jpg. This file is in the public domain because it has been released by the Los Angeles County Museum of Art. Accessed May 29, 2016

[25] Pingstone, Adrian. "Royal Crescent (Bath, England)." File:Royal.crescent.aerial.bath.arp.jpg, Wikipedia , 24 Oct. 2005, https://en.wikipedia.org/wiki/file%3aroyal.crescent.aerial.bath.arp.jpg. Photographed by Adrian Pingstone and placed in the public domain.

[26] Josh83. "Hamburg after the 1943 Firestorm." JoshuaAndAndrew, Blogspot, http://joshuaandandrew.blogspot.ca/2011/01/frightening-hamburg-firestorm.html.

[27] Wikipedia contributors. "The Pax Program." Wikipedia, Wikipedia, the Free Encyclopedia. , 15 Aug. 2016, https://en.wikipedia.org/wiki/the_pax_program.

[28] "Menno Simons." File:Menno Simonsz.gif, Wikimedia Commons, 9 July 2009, https://commons.wikimedia.org/wiki/file:menno_simonsz.gif. This work is in the public domain in its country of origin and other countries and areas where the copyright term is the author's life plus 70 years or less.

[29] Siemens, Alfred Henry. *Mennonite Settlement in the Lower Fraser Valley*. Unpublished M.A. thesis, Department of Geography, University of British Columbia. 1960.

[30] United Kingdom Government. "Cologne 1945 5." File:Cologne 1945 5.Jpg, Wikipedia Foundation, 31 Mar. 2006, https://en.wikipedia.org/wiki/file:cologne_1945_5.jpg. This work is in the public domain worldwide. This is because: It is a photograph created by the United Kingdom Government taken prior to 1 June 1957.

[31] Norberg, Heidi L. "Bob Detweiler's Obituary in the AJC." VirusHead, Virushead, 4 Sept. 2008, http://www.virushead.net/vhrandom/2008/09/bob-detweilers-obituary-in-the-ajc/. August 2016, Image is used with permission of author.

[32] Personal communication. Edwin Hintz to Siemens, January 1, 1955

[33] Siemens, Alfred. "Mitteilungen aus Deutschland" *Mennonitische Rundschau*. December 8, 1954, p. 3.

[34] Thiessen, Bernhard, editor. "Mennonite Community of Hamburg and Altona ." Mennonite Community of Hamburg and Altona, Mennonite community of Hamburg and Altona, http://www.mennoniten-hamburg.de/. Accessed August 2016

[35] jpc Passion for Music. "Karl Sundermeier Der Orchideenmissionar." Jpc Passion for Music, jpc, https://www.jpc.de/jpcng/books/detail/-/art/sieglinde-quick-karl-sundermeier-der-orchideenmissionar/hnum/5147027.

[36] Houghton, Frank. *Quiet Time: An Inter-Varsity Guidebook for Devotions Pamphlet*. Inter-Varsity Press, 1945. p. 24.

[37] Bakewell, Sarah. *How to Live—or—a Life of Montaigne: in One Question and Twenty Attempts at an Answer*. New York: Other Press, 2010. p.2.

[38] Miller, James. *Examined Lives: from Socrates to Nietzsche*. New York: Farrar, Straus and Giroux, 2011. p. 192.

[39] Plumtree. "Lüneburger Heide Im März." File:Heide 14 Wiki.jpg, Wikimedia Commons, 19 Dec. 2005, https://commons.wikimedia.org/wiki/file:heide_14_wiki.jpg.

[40] Wikipedia contributors. "Lüneburg Heath." Wikipedia, the Free Encyclopedia. Wikipedia, the Free Encyclopedia, 6 Aug. 2016. Web. 1 Sep. 2016.

[41] Siemens, Alfred H. *Una manera de ver: LOS TUXTLAS*. México, CONABIO, 2009.

[42] Below, Ernst. *Mexiko: Skizzen Und Typen Aus Dem Italien Der Neuen Welt*. Berlin, Allgemeiner Verein für Deutsche Litteratur, 1899.

[43] Anonymous. "Citrus Natsudaidai." File:Citrus Natsudaidai Melanose.jpg, Wikimedia Commons, 26 May 2008, https://commons.wikimedia.org/wiki/file:citrus_natsudaidai_melanose.jpg. OK to use: GFDL&CC, No author or source. Accessed May 29, 2016

[44] Ackroyd, Peter. *Venice: Pure City*. New York: Nan A. Talese/Doubleday, 2009. p. 289.

[45] Ibid, p. 357.

[46] Bartolomeo, Fra. "Portrait of Girolamo Savonarola 1497." File:Girolamo Savonarola.jpg, Wikimedia Commons, San Marco, Florence, 7 Dec. 2009, https://commons.wikimedia.org/wiki/file:girolamo_savonarola.jpg. Anonymous. "Hanging and Burning of Girolamo Savonarola 1498." File:Hanging and Burning of Girolamo Savonarola in Florence.jpg, Wikimdeia Commons, Florence, Italy, 18 Sept. 2006, https://commons.wikimedia.org/wiki/file:hanging_and_burning_of_girolamo_savonarola_in_florence.jpg. The official position taken by the Wikimedia Foundation is that "faithful reproductions of two-dimensional public domain works of art are public domain". This photographic reproduction is therefore also considered to be in the public domain in the United States. In other jurisdictions, re-use of this content may be restricted; see Reuse of PD-Art. Accessed May 29, 2016

[47] Unna, Jörg Bittner. "'Atlas Slave' by Michelangelo 1520." File:'Atlas Slave' by Michelangelo - JBU 02.Jpg, Wikimdeia Commons, 23 Aug. 2011, https://commons.wikimedia.org/wiki/file:%27atlas_slave%27_by_michelangelo_-_jbu_02.jpg. Accessed May 29, 2016

[48] Yair, Haklai. "Torso Del Belvedere." File:Belvedere Torso-Vatican Museums-2.Jpg, Wikimedia Commons, 2 Oct. 2009, https://commons.wikimedia.org/wiki/file:belvedere_torso-vatican_museums-2.jpg. Accessed May 29, 2016

[49] Siemens, Alfred H. "Prehistoric Water and Land Management." *Water for the Future: Water Resources Developments in Perspective*. Rotterdam: Balkema. 1987, pp. 139–151.

[50] Damato, Alessio. "Chiesa Gesu Facade." File:Chiesa Gesu Facade.jpg, Wikipedia, 21 Aug. 2007, https://en.wikipedia.org/wiki/file:chiesa_gesu_facade.jpg. Accessed May 29, 2016

[51] Solntsev, Yegor. "Gulf of Naples (1850's)." File:Yegor Solntsev, Gulf of Naples.jpg, Wikimedia, Russia, 23 Sept. 2010, https://commons.wikimedia.org/wiki/file:yegor_solntsev,_gulf_of_naples.jpg. Accessed May 29, 2016

[52] 92bari. "Olive Tree «Cima Di Bitonto» in Puglia – Italia." File:Ulivobitonto.gif, Wikimedia Commons, 28 Oct. 2007, https://commons.wikimedia.org/wiki/file:ulivobitonto.gif. Accessed May 29, 2016

[53] UNESCO World Heritage Centre. "The Trulli of Alberobello." World Heritage Centre, UNESCO, 1996, http://whc.unesco.org/en/list/787. Accessed May 29, 2016

[54] van Mierlo, Frank. "Corinth Canal." File:Corinth Canal by Frank Van Mierlo.jpg, Wikimedia Commons, 30 Sept. 2010, https://commons.wikimedia.org/wiki/file:corinth_canal_by_frank_van_mierlo.jpg. Accessed May 29, 2016

[55] artsandletters. "Contemporary Aerial View of the Acropolis." From the Heart of Darkness, Blog, 21 Nov. 2010, http://theancientworld.tumblr.com/search/acropolis+aerial. Accessed May 29, 2016

[56] Savin, A. "View of Athens." File:Attica 06-13 Athens 22 View from Acropolis Hill - Museum of Ancient Agora.jpg, Wikimedia Commons, 3 Aug. 2013, https://commons.wikimedia.org/wiki/file:attica_06-13_athens_22_view_from_acropolis_hill_-_museum_of_ancient_agora.jpg. Accessed May 29, 2016

Gertjan, R. "Inside the Stoa of Attalus." File:Interior Stoa of Attalus 2.Jpg, Wikimedia Commons, 17 Apr. 2011, https://commons.wikimedia.org/wiki/file:interior_stoa_of_attalus_2.jpg. Accessed May 29, 2016

[57] Fleming, Chris. "Temple of Zeus." File:Temple of Zeus in Athens 079.Jpg, Wikimedia Commons, 15 Jan. 2006, https://commons.wikimedia.org/wiki/file:temple_of_zeus_in_athens_079.jpg. Accessed May 29, 2016

[58] Ggia. "The Venetian Fortress Koule." File:20090415 Hrakleio Krhth Limani Koules 1.Jpg, Wikimedia Commons, 18 Apr. 2009, https://commons.wikimedia.org/wiki/file:20090415_hrakleio_krhth_limani_koules_1.jpg. Accessed May 29, 2016

[59] Ackroyd, Peter. *Venice: Pure City*. New York: Nan A. Talese/Doubleday, 2009.

[60] Unknown author. "Fresco of Bull-Leaping from Knossos." File:Knossos Bull.jpg, Wikipedia, Crete, date unknown, https://en.wikipedia.org/wiki/file:knossos_bull.jpg. Accessed May 29, 2016

[61] Kabel, Matthias. "Greek Vase with Runners at the Panathenaic Games." File:Greek Vase with Runners at the Panathenaic Games 530 BC.jpg, Wikimedia Commons, 28 Jan. 2006, https://commons.wikimedia.org/wiki/file:greek_vase_with_runners_at_the_panathenaic_games_530_bc.jpg. Accessed May 29, 2016

[62] von Daphni, Meister. "Mosaiken Der Kirche Von Daphni." File:Meister Von Daphni 002.Jpg, Wikimedia Commons, Klosterkirche, Daphni, 20 May 2005, https://commons.wikimedia.org/wiki/file:meister_von_daphni_002.jpg?uselang=en-ca. circa 1100. Accessed May 29, 2016

[63] Urban. "Corinthe Temple." File: Corinthe1.Jpg, Wikimedia Commons, 6 Feb. 2005, https://commons.wikimedia.org/wiki/file:corinthe1.jpg. Accessed May 29, 2016

[64] Trepte, Andreas. "The Lion Gate at Mycenae." File: Lions-Gate-Mycenae.jpg, Wikimedia Commons, 7 Jan. 2008, https://commons.wikimedia.org/wiki/file:lions-gate-mycenae.jpg. Accessed May 29, 2016

[65] Carolsfeld, Julius Schnorr Von. *Die Bibel in Bildern*. Leipzig, 1852.

[66] United Nations. "Map of Former Yugoslavia." File:Former Yugoslavia Map.png, Wikimedia Commons, 10 Mar. 2007, https://commons.wikimedia.org/wiki/file:former_yugoslavia_map.png. This image is a map derived from a United Nations map. Unless stated otherwise, UN maps are to be considered in the public domain. This applies worldwide. Accessed May 29, 2016

[67] Wikipedia. http://commons.wikimedia.org/wiki/File:Red_star.svg This image of simple geometry is ineligible for copyright and therefore in the public domain, because it consists entirely of information that is common property and contains no original authorship

[68] Raphael. "Madonna Im Grünen, Szene: Maria Mit Christuskind Und Johannes Dem Täufer." Kunsthistorisches Museum, Vienna, Austria, 1506. Accessed May 29, 2016

[69] Rembrandt. "Self-Portrait with Beret." *File: Rembrandt Harmensz. Van Rijn 132.Jpg*, Wikimedia Commons, Vienna, 2 June 2014, https://commons.wikimedia.org/wiki/file:rembrandt_harmensz._van_rijn_132.jpg. Accessed May 29, 2016

[70] Rubens, Peter Paul. "Het Toilet Van Venus." *File:Rubens Venus at a Mirror c1615.Jpg*, Wikimedia, Wenen, 29 Dec. 2010, https://commons.wikimedia.org/wiki/file:rubens_venus_at_a_mirror_c1615.jpg. Accessed May 29, 2016

[71] van Ruisdael, Jacob. "The Windmill at Wijk Bij Duurstede." *File:The Windmill at Wijk Bij Duurstede 1670 Ruisdael.jpg*, Wikimedia Commons, Amsterdam, 10 May 2012, https://en.wikipedia.org/wiki/file:the_windmill_at_wijk_bij_duurstede_1670_ruisdael.jpg. Accessed May 29, 2016

[72] Bruegel the Elder, Pieter. "Monthly Cycle, Scene: The Hunters in the Snow (January)." *File:Pieter Bruegel d. Ä. 106b.Jpg*, Wikipedia, Vienna, 29 Sept. 2008, https://en.wikipedia.org/wiki/file:pieter_bruegel_d._%c3%84._106b.jpg. Accessed May 29, 2016

[73] Fotoatelier des KHM. "Wagenburg, Blick in Die Schauhalle." File:Wagenburg Blick in Die Schauhalle.jpg, Wikimedia Commons, 4 Oct. 2006, https://commons.wikimedia.org/wiki/file:wagenburg_blick_in_die_schauhalle.jpg. Accessed May 29, 2016

[74] Xaver, Franz. "Edelweiß Leontopodium Alpinum." File:Leontopodium alpinum1.Jpg, Wikimedia Commons, Aug. 1989, https://en.wikipedia.org/wiki/file%3aleontopodium_alpinum1.jpg. Accessed May 29, 2016

[75] Siemens, Alfred H. *Reading my mother's diaries*. Unpublished. 2004. Personal materials.

[76] Bossi, Andrew. "View from Monk Hill, Salzburg, Austria." File:1907 - Salzburg - View from Mönchsberg.JPG, Wikimedia Commons, 6 July 2007, https://commons.wikimedia.org/wiki/file:1907_-_salzburg_-_view_from_m%c3%b6nchsberg.jpg?uselang=en-ca. Accessed May 29, 2016

[77] michaelXXLF. "Eingang Zur Wieskirche." File:Wies Eingang.jpg, Wikimedia Commons, 21 Aug. 2005, https://commons.wikimedia.org/wiki/file:wies_eingang.jpg. Accessed May 29, 2016

Behringer, B. "Wieskirche." File:Wieskirche Ansicht.JPG, Wikimedia Commons, 26 May 2007, https://commons.wikimedia.org/wiki/file:wieskirche_ansicht.jpg. Accessed May 29, 2016

[78] Marcellin, Maurice. "Rosario Chapel in Santo Domingo Church." File:Capilla Rosario Puebla.jpg, Wikimedia Commons, 18 Aug. 2006, https://commons.wikimedia.org/wiki/file:capilla_rosario_puebla.jpg. Accessed May 29, 2016

[79] . Stein, Peter. "Fortress Ruins of the Hohentwiel." File: Hohentwiel-Luftbild.jpg, Wikimedia Commons, 2000, https://commons.wikimedia.org/wiki/file:hohentwiel-luftbild.jpg. Accessed May 29, 2016

[80] LoKiLeCh. "Blick Von Neuschwanstein." File:Neuschwanstein Fernblick pano2.Jpg, Wikimedia Commons, 7 Sept. 2008, https://commons.wikimedia.org/wiki/file:neuschwanstein_fernblick_pano2.jpg. Accessed May 29, 2016

[81] Karwath, Andre. "This Image Shows the Pfahlbau Museum Unteruhldingen, Germany with Reconstructed Stilt Houses Based on Different Archaeological Finds." File:Pile-Dwelling Museum Unteruhldingen (Aka).Jpg, Wikimedia Commons, 18 Aug. 2007, https://commons.wikimedia.org/wiki/file:pile-dwelling_museum_unteruhldingen_(aka).jpg?uselang=en-ca. Accessed May 29, 2016

[82] Meyer, Wilhelm. "Ulrich Zwingli." The Catholic Encyclopedia. Vol. 15. New York: Robert Appleton Company, 1912. New Advent website accessed 29 May 2016. http://www.newadvent.org/cathen/15772a.htm

[83] Arminia. "Black Forest in Southwestern Germany." File:Blick Über Den Mittleren Schwarzwald 2.JPG, Wikimedia Commons, 3 Apr. 2004, https://commons.wikimedia.org/wiki/file:blick_%c3%bcber_den_mittleren_schwarzwald_2.jpg. Accessed May 29, 2016

[84] Hutter, Alfred. "Speyer Cathedral." File:Speyer—Cathedral—South-View—(Gentry).Jpg, Wikipedia, 31 Aug. 2008, https://en.wikipedia.org/wiki/file%3aspeyer---cathedral---south-view---(gentry).jpg. Accessed May 29, 2016

[85] Wofl. "Speyerer Dom, Blick Von Der Empore." File:Speyerer Dom Mittelschiff.jpg, Wikimedia Commons, 11 Sept. 2005, https://commons.wikimedia.org/wiki/file:speyerer_dom_mittelschiff.jpg. Accessed May 29, 2016

[86] Cranach the Elder, Lukas. "Martin Luther." Wikipedia, Wikimedia Foundation, Augsburg, 2005, https://commons.wikimedia.org/wiki/file:martin_luther,_1529.jpg. Accessed May 29, 2016

[87] Cosmicgirl. "Statue of Roland in Wedel." File: Roland in Wedel.JPG, Wikimedia Commons, May 2007, https://commons.wikimedia.org/wiki/file:roland_in_wedel.jpg. Accessed May 29, 2016

Wikipedia contributors. "Wedel." Wikipedia, the Free Encyclopedia. Wikipedia, the Free Encyclopedia, 17 Jun. 2015. Web. 1 Sep. 2016.

[88] Carolsfeld, Julius Schnorr Von. *Die Bibel in Bildern*. Leipzig, 1852.

[89] "Emblem of the Wandervogel Movement (1905)." File:Wandervogel Greif.svg, Wikimedia Commons, 21 Sept. 2007, https://commons.wikimedia.org/wiki/file:wandervogel_greif.svg. This work is in the public domain in its country of origin and other countries and areas where the copyright term is the author's life plus 70 years or less. Accessed May 29, 2016

[90] Wikipedia contributors. "Wandervogel." Wikipedia, The Free Encyclopedia. Wikipedia, The Free Encyclopedia, 14 Jul. 2016. Web. 1 Sep. 2016.

[91] Rudofsky, Bernard. *Architecture without Architects; an Introduction to Non-Pedigreed Architecture*. New York, Museum of modern art, 1964.

[92] Film Fan. "Theatrical Poster for the Film Rear Window." File:Rear Window Film Poster.jpg, Wikimedia Commons, 22 Apr. 2012, https://en.wikipedia.org/wiki/file%3arearwindowposter.jpg. This work is in the public domain because it was published in the United States between 1923 and 1963 and although there may or may not have been a copyright notice, the copyright was not renewed. Accessed May 29, 2016

[93] Offizielles Wochenprogramm vom 16.12.1954-31.12.1954. From margin of map published for Fremdenverkehrs (tourists) - und Kongress-Zentrale Hamburg e.V. Author's personal materials. AHS

[94] Schulz, Günter T. in *Das Ist Hamburg: Aquarelle Hamburger Künstler*. Tegtmeier, Konrad (eds) Hamburg, Sattelmair, 1954. p. 49

[95] No Author. "Hamburg Places: Jungfernstieg." *Hamburg Places: Jungfernstieg*, hamburgtravelguide, http://hamburgtravelguide.com/hamburg-jungfernstieg.html. N.d.

[96] Studt, Bernhard und Hans Olsen. Unser kleines Hamburgbuch. Hans Köhler Verlag, Hamburg 1957.

[97] Thubron, Colin. "Mesmerized by Germany." *The New York Review of Books*, 19 Dec. 2013, p. 67.

[98] Husmann, Fritz in *Das Ist Hamburg: Aquarelle Hamburger Künstler*. Tegtmeier, Konrad (eds) Hamburg, Sattelmair, 1954. p. 47

[99] Houston, J. M. *A Social Geography of Europe*. London: Duckworth, 1953.

[100] Wikipedia contributors. "Icelandic Airlines." Wikipedia, the Free Encyclopedia. Wikipedia, the Free Encyclopedia, 18 May. 2016. Web. 1 Sep. 2016.

[101] Turgenjew, Iwan S. *Väter. Und Söhne*. München: Goldmann, 1955.

CPSIA information can be obtained
at www.ICGtesting.com
Printed in the USA
LVHW070243230721
693489LV00015B/315